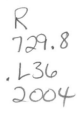
Leading a Patient-Safe Organization

Your board, staff, or clients may also benefit from this book's insight. For more information on quantity discounts, contact the Health Administration Press Marketing Manager at (312) 424-9470.

This publication is intended to provide accurate and authoritative information in regard to the subject matter covered. It is sold, or otherwise provided, with the understanding that the publisher is not engaged in rendering professional services. If professional advice or other expert assistance is required, the services of a competent professional should be sought.

The statements and opinions contained in this book are strictly those of the author(s) and do not represent the official positions of the American College of Healthcare Executives or of the Foundation of the American College of Healthcare Executives.

Library of Congress Cataloging-in-Publication Data

Lambert, Matthew J.
     Leading a patient-safe organization / Matthew J. Lambert.
          p. cm.
     Includes bibliographical references.
     ISBN 1-56793-230-4 (alk. paper)
     1. Medical errors—Prevention. 2. Medical care—Quality control. 3. Medicine—Practice—Safety measures.
     4. Health facilities—Quality control. I. Title

R729.8.L36 2004
362.11'608—dc22

2004049127

The paper used in this publication meets the minimum requirements of American National Standard for Information Sciences—Permanence of Paper for Printed Library Materials, ANSI Z39.48-1984. ∞ ™

Acquisitions editor: Audrey Kaufman; Project manager: Jane C. Williams; Layout editor: Amanda J. Karvelaitis; Cover design: Anne Locascio

Health Administration Press
A division of the Foundation of the
   American College of Healthcare Executives
1 North Franklin Street, Suite 1700
Chicago, IL 60606-4425
(312) 424-2800

Introduction

Perhaps the most significant challenge facing healthcare executives today is the public's loss of confidence in the ability of healthcare organizations to deliver safe care.

Five years have passed since the Institute of Medicine (IOM) published *To Err Is Human: Building a Safer Health System*, a report that documents the pervasiveness of medical errors and the cost of such mistakes in human lives and organizational resources. Some healthcare insiders and observers felt that the initial clamor about the IOM report would lose steam and be replaced by other, more pressing issues, but that did not occur. Federal and state governments, regulatory and accrediting agencies, payers, employers, and the public continue to demand more reporting of healthcare outcomes and greater accountability from healthcare organizations for eliminating medical mistakes. The persistence of flawed processes and inept practitioners—factors that lead to errors and thus scrutiny of physicians and healthcare systems—is a major impediment to attempts to ameliorate the high cost of medical liability insurance and to generate support for tort reform.

Thomas Kuhn (1996) popularized the term "paradigms" and defined it as those "universally recognized scientific achievements that provide model problems and solutions to a community of practitioners." New paradigms emerge only after current theories fail to solve problems.

The failure of existing systems to address and minimize medical error has led us to a new paradigm—that of public accountability for medical outcomes and for focusing on eliminating error. The fragmented nature of the healthcare industry means that the immediate responsibility for improving outcomes and minimizing adverse events falls to individual organizations and their leaders, including board members, healthcare executives, nurses, and physicians.

Members of our communities rely on us to help them stay healthy for as long as possible. They come when they are sick; they seek comfort when they are dying. They trust that we adhere to the dictum *primum non nocere*—first do no harm. Our mission as healthcare providers is to serve as best we can while continuing our journey to improve patient care.

This book is written for senior healthcare executives. It provides essential information that may guide leaders in improving quality of care and patient safety in their organizations. The book is divided into three chapters:

- Chapter 1: The basics of medical error are presented.
- Chapter 2: The role of leadership in addressing the problem of medical error and adverse outcomes is examined.
- Chapter 3: The chapter discusses the development of a culture that ensures that potential and actual errors are identified and corrected and that the environment is continuously strengthened to promote patient safety and desired outcomes.

REFERENCE

Kuhn, T. 1996. *The Structure of Scientific Revolutions*. Chicago: University of Chicago Press.

CHAPTER 1

Medical **Error**

Ernst Mach said, "Knowledge and error flow from the same mental sources, only success can tell one from the other" (Reason 1990, 1).

There are abundant opportunities for errors to occur in the complex world of modern medical care. The selection of a particular diagnostic or therapeutic procedure may not be indicated, may be unsound, or may be inappropriate. All procedures and medications are associated with recognized complications or side effects. Nosocomial infections acquired by some patients may be abetted by inappropriate administration of antibiotics or failure to observe simple hygienic measures such as hand washing. The euphemism "therapeutic misadventure" encompasses errors ranging from a surgeon cutting off the wrong extremity to a nurse giving the wrong dose of medication. ▶

Most healthcare observers concede that errors identified in U.S. hospitals are only a portion of those that occur overall. Other healthcare delivery sites—such as physician offices, clinics, and ambulatory surgical centers—have less oversight and thus may likely find errors to be even more prevalent (Hayward and Hofer 2001; Kohn, Corrigan, and Donaldson 2000). These problems are not confined to the United States. A study of British and Australian hospitals revealed that between 11 and 17 percent of patients experienced an adverse event, about half of which were judged preventable if ordinary standards of care were employed (Vincent, Neale, and Woloshynowych 2001).

Of concern are preventable adverse events and those associated with negligence (see Sidebar A for the definitions). Not all adverse events are attributable to individual incompetence or carelessness. The cultures of medicine and nursing, however, are largely responsible for people's tendency to view errors as individual failures, and a vigorous tort system continues to link liability to individual decision making.

The good news for healthcare and for most other human endeavors is that correct actions far outweigh mistakes. The fact is that individuals, when operating alone, are very reliable.

Many errors in healthcare, as in other industries, occur when people interact unsuccessfully with technology or complex systems. The design of such technology and systems may not adequately take into account the way in which people perceive, think, and act. This may result in unexpected incompatibilities that lead to errors (Casey 1993, 9).

This chapter explores the types of errors commonly encountered in healthcare. It also makes a case for viewing mistakes in a systems framework rather than as an individual fault.

FRAMEWORKS FOR UNDERSTANDING ERROR

A number of conceptual frameworks have been developed that explain the types of human error. One theory is the division of human actions into three categories—skill based, rule based, and knowledge based:

- *Skill-based actions* involve carrying out fairly routine, repetitive tasks largely automatically. Periodic

<aside>

SIDEBAR A

An *error* is...the failure of a planned action to be completed as intended...or the use of a wrong plan to achieve an aim....

An *adverse event* is an injury caused by medical management rather than the underlying condition of the patient. An adverse event attributable to error is a "preventable adverse event."

Negligent adverse events represent a subset of preventable adverse events that satisfy legal criteria used in determining negligence... (Kohn, Corrigan, and Donaldson 2000).

</aside>

checks are done to ensure the process is proceeding correctly.

- *Rule-based actions* are employed when rules that are either written down or memorized must be applied. They are of the "if/then" type: *If* a certain situation is present, *then* a certain procedure is used. In many cases, the situation has been encountered before or it is covered by a rule.
- *Knowledge-based actions* are used when existing solutions do not work or when the situation is so novel that it does not fit any of the preprogrammed solutions available. This requires the use of existing knowledge and conscious analytical processes. It is the most difficult of the actions because often people's knowledge of the situation is incomplete, their capacity to hold information is limited, and they have no opportunity to try a variety of different solutions because a decision must be made in a timely fashion (Reason 1997).

Mistakes (see Sidebar B) can be rule based or knowledge based. Knowledge-base mistakes arise when available solutions are not adequate and when information must be synthesized to generate a new course of action. Rule-based errors occur when correct rules are misapplied, when incorrect rules are used, or when a correct rule is violated (Reason 1997, 71).

When violations occur, the policy or procedure must be reexamined to ensure that it is not so rigid that it must be routinely violated to enable work to get done (e.g., a policy that forbids nurses to accept verbal orders) or that it cannot be followed because of environmental circumstances (e.g., too few RNs work on a unit that has a policy on nurse-patient ratios). The development of even stricter policies after an adverse outcome is often a knee-jerk reaction, preceding any in-depth analysis of the event and the contributing factors. The rationale behind this seems to be that the existing policy was too loose; thus, if it is made less flexible, further errors cannot occur. An existing policy may need to be modified, but making it more rigid can make compliance impossible and a bad situation worse. In addition, such a quick fix provides a false sense of security that the problem has been addressed and that further errors can be prevented.

Latent and Active Errors

Most errors identified in healthcare are of the active variety, and their effects may be noted within a relatively short period. These *active errors* mostly involve healthcare practitioners who interact directly with the patient, such as a physician making a technical mistake during surgery or a nurse administering an incorrect medication.

Latent errors, on the other hand, are usually far removed from the healthcare practitioner and the patient. These are difficult to detect unless a particular event or near miss is thoroughly investigated. According to Kohn, Corrigan, and Donaldson (2000, 55–56), latent errors

- may be present in machines or devices as a result of design flaws;
- may result from poorly designed policies and procedures, administrative decisions about staffing or purchasing, or many other like factors; and
- may only be exposed when accompanied by other circumstances that might not have been anticipated to occur at the same time.

In 1987, the King's Cross Underground (subway) fire in London killed 31 people. The fire began in rubbish and grease in the running track of an escalator, probably as a

result of a discarded cigarette. Some of the latent factors identified after the review included the presence of wooden escalators, the failure to install smoke alarms because of cost constraints, the lack of attention to the regular cleaning of debris from the escalator as a result of the blurring of maintenance and cleaning responsibilities, the lack of an evacuation plan, and the inadequate fire and emergency training of staff. If the outcome of this investigation had been simply to clean the escalators more frequently, other, more substantial latent defects would have persisted and perhaps aggravated the loss of life if a fire from another source occurred (Reason 1990, 257).

In short, the identification and remediation of latent errors is more difficult. But, in the long run, it may be more important to patient safety than simply dealing with the proximate cause of a mistake.

The interconnectedness of latent failures, active errors, and a breakdown of defenses results in adverse outcomes. More often than not, an analysis of an adverse event does not reveal that an incompetent person was responsible. Rather, it suggests that a well-meaning person was involved in a situation or activity that was error prone because of

So why are people so ready to accept human error as an explanation for an adverse event rather than performing an in-depth analysis? The answer is deeply rooted in human nature. Psychologists call it the *fundamental attribution error*. When we see or hear of someone performing badly, we attribute this to some enduring aspect of the individual's personality.... But if you were to ask the person in question why they are behaving in this fashion, they would almost certainly point to the local situation and say that they had no choice.... The reality, of course, lies somewhere in between (Reason 1997, 126–27).

design or system deficiencies (Spath 2000, 6).

THE SYSTEMS NATURE OF ERROR

An idea that has been around in other industries for years is the role of poorly designed systems in creating error. The recent focus on medical error has caused this concept to be emphasized within healthcare. But it is difficult for healthcare professionals to let go of the notion that someone is responsible for every adverse medical outcome (see Sidebar C).

According to Moray (1994, 67–71), a *system* can be defined as a collection of regularly interacting or interdependent items (including people) designed to accomplish a particular goal or purpose. If the entire system is designed correctly, then errors should be infrequent. The systems approach to error management suggests that the source of errors can be traced to the design of equipment, procedures, processes, and activities coupled with patterns of human behavior. Hospitals that seek to reduce medical error need to emphasize this approach and eliminate the tendency to punish

those who make mistakes. The following is a summary of this view (Moray 1994, 67–91):

- A punitive culture is counterproductive. It is likely to drive mistakes underground and lead to underreporting or covering up of errors.
- Thinking systematically about medical error is recognizing that relatively few mistakes can be attributed solely to individual actions.
- When focusing on reducing medical error, the entire organization should be viewed as a system that operates and interacts in complex ways. It includes physicians, nurses, employees, equipment, policies, procedures, physical plant, and many other components.
- Medical error is minimized when the system is designed optimally and the interrelationships between system components are understood.

In some respects, the system approach demands more of healthcare providers. They have a responsibility to actively participate in efforts to develop systems and processes that improve patient care and safety (Richardson and Corrigan 2003).

HEALTHCARE AS A SYSTEM

The system in healthcare is messy and dynamic in its relationships, the strength and quality of the interactions, the way human illness unfolds from person to person, and the fact that complications sometimes result from attempted solutions (Weick 2002, 177–78).

The hospital can be thought of as a system of sorts, with all the individual departments and their activities as subsystems that can be broken down for more productive analysis. Often missed is how critical interrelationships between these many areas can contribute to medical error and adverse outcomes. Human error in this systemic view is considered the consequence of interconnected factors. This offers a much broader array of influences and moves away from the actions of one individual (Bogner 1994, 377–78).

Solving the error problem would be a good deal easier if healthcare is delivered in a stepwise and predictable fashion. One could then isolate the process that is out of sync and correct it. But healthcare has many characteristics of a complex system, including the following (Perrow 1999, 72–89):

- Processes are highly specialized and interdependent.
- Many feedback loops are involved that generate additional, and sometimes unanticipated, responses.
- Information may be derived indirectly.
- Resources (including people) cannot be easily substituted because of their degree of specialization.

Tight and Loose Coupling of Systems

Another factor in medical error is how processes interact with one another.

Tightly coupled systems have little slack between sequences: when one is activated, another follows immediately. Turning on an IV pump, for example, initiates the flow of medication into a patient. An error with the rate of flow or with the dose or type of medication may have an immediate effect on the patient that cannot be aborted.

Contrast this with loosely coupled systems. In deleting a file from a computer, for example, you would first receive a warning that asks if you are sure about your action before the process is initiated. This allows you to recover from a potential mistake before any damage is done (Perrow 1999, 89–100).

Building in safeguards that make error less likely or recovery more possible make tightly coupled processes, such as medication administration and surgical procedures, more reliable (Kohn, Corrigan, and Donaldson 2000). The Joint Commission on Accreditation of Healthcare Organizations's (JCAHO) protocol for preventing wrong-site surgery involves marking the surgical site, involving the patient in the marking process, and taking a final "time out" in the operating room to double check information with all members of the surgical team (JCAHO 2003).

RECONCILING THE SYSTEM AND HUMAN CAUSES OF ERROR

The concept of the systems approach to viewing error should be reconciled with the more pervasive view of individual responsibility. Complex systems can break down at many points as the result of latent and active failures (see Figure 1 on the following page) (Reason 1990, 202).

Role of Fallible Decisions
The origin of many errors is fallible decisions. In healthcare, the continued pressure on organizational finances has led to a number of faulty choices that affect employees and resources. These include curtailing overtime and agency use, reducing staff, substituting registered nurses with less-skilled employees, and deferring equipment upgrades. Often the results of such changes are readily visible in the next quarter's financial statements, but the effects on patient safety and healthcare outcomes are more subtle.

The incidence of nosocomial infections may increase, lengths of stay may rise, more patients may suffer from decubitus ulcers, and medication errors may be more frequent. But these occurrences may not appear on management's radar screen until they reach significant levels or lead to a major adverse outcome. In fact, the news of improved financial performance may reinforce fallible strategies and push patient safety initiatives further into the background.

Impact of Middle Management
Middle managers have a great deal to do with the quality of staff recruited and retained, the degree to which policies and procedures are implemented, the types of activities emphasized and rewarded, and the

Figure 1. Human Contribution to System Breakdowns

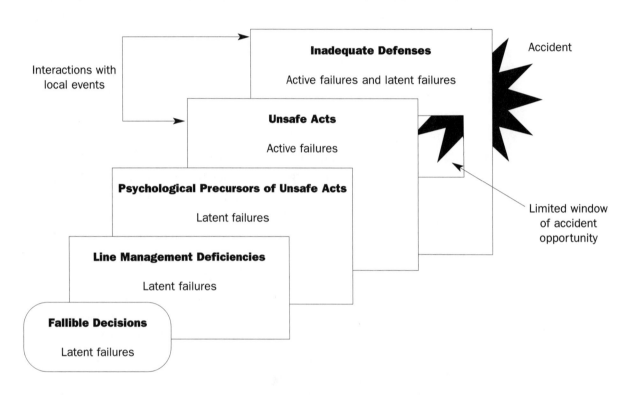

Source: Reason, J. 1990. From *Human Error,* Figure 7.5, p. 202. Reprinted with permission of Cambridge University Press.

method by which organizational initiatives are interpreted to frontline staff. This is perhaps the most difficult position in healthcare administration. Managers feel the pressure from top executives, especially when the organization's financial picture is bleak.

Under such scrutiny, the manager may make less-than-optimal decisions about resource allocation, especially staffing. This decision can be reflected by a decline in patient satisfaction and an increase in adverse patient outcomes. The manager may also feel the impact of a fatigued and demoralized workforce, who works with limited resources. Such employees are unlikely to put forth their best efforts and may be more careless. In fact, they may develop a mindset that adverse outcomes are not their problem but the responsibility of management.

Swiss Cheese Effect

The system nature of accidents can best be understood by a "Swiss cheese" diagram. Figure 2 shows how latent and active errors are present in the multiple layers of safeguards of a policy or procedure and how such defects must line up for an error to reach a patient (Reason 1990, 208). Awareness of how deficiencies in each of these defensive layers contributes to an adverse outcome can facilitate the development of necessary feedback loops, which will identify and correct defects.

COMMUNICATION AND RISK MANAGEMENT

Improving communication seems to be part of any solution to a persistent healthcare issue. Senior management

Figure 2. Factors in Fallible, High-Level Decision Making

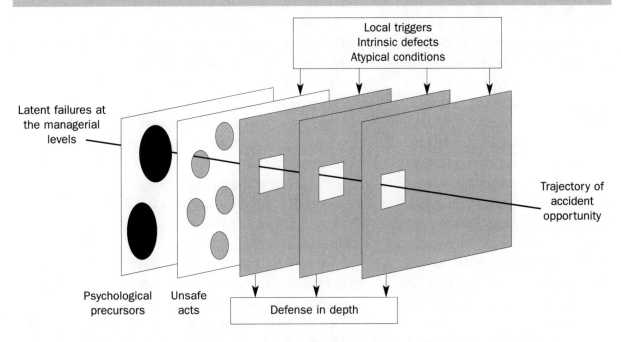

Source: Reason, J. 1990. From *Human Error*, Figure 7.6, p. 208. Reprinted with permission of Cambridge University Press.

must be confident that a mechanism is in place for receiving regular feedback regarding the impact of their strategic and tactical decisions on the incidence of medical errors and adverse outcomes. An organization truly committed to patient safety analyzes every decision's impact on patient care before implementing that decision.

A vigorous risk management program is an essential component of any effort to reduce errors. The goal of risk management is to conserve the financial resources of the organization by identifying adverse outcomes and limiting the economic damage of any litigation. Risk management, however, should be structured more broadly and should be part of all efforts to improve patient safety and outcomes, including all sentinel event investigations and root cause analyses.

The risk manager must interact with staff on a regular basis, not only to seek information about adverse outcomes and near misses but also to provide educational opportunities to help staff do their job better. Information developed by the risk management department should be reported on a regular basis to the organization at large, to senior management, and to the board of trustees. The latter group, of course, is most interested in cases dealing with substantial liability, but it should also be educated on all risk-reduction efforts.

PREVENTABLE ERRORS

Errors in healthcare are inevitable, but some can be prevented. One of the more devastating preventable mistakes is the inadvertent administration of concentrated potassium chloride in lieu of a lower concentration of potassium or another medication. Such high-concentration medications are often kept on the nursing units with other commonly used and safer medicine. By removing such solutions from patient care areas, such errors are avoided.

Another change that is necessary is making tubing or tank connections to containers that carry different substances incompatible with one another. This is especially important in the operating room, where oxygen and nitrous oxide tanks sit side by side.

We need to look for more of these opportunities to make changes that prevent errors. Although significant progress has been made, much needs to be done.

THE BLESSING AND CURSE OF TECHNOLOGY

In many industries, technology has replaced human beings. The auto industry is a great example, with its use of robotics in car assembly. What used to require human judgment and decision making does not any longer, although human intervention is still required occasionally, especially in monitoring the equipment to ensure that it is running normally. A worker must still know the technology to the degree that he or she can identify problems before they lead to a disaster. But is this something on which we can rely?

The problem with many technical malfunctions is that they are uncommon and may be unusual. Workers may have never experienced such an event and may not recognize it, or if it is recognized, they may be unsure about how to respond. Faced with a malfunction, staff may develop a theory of its cause based on past experiences with other technology and may adhere to this concept even as the situation deteriorates (Chiles 2001, 63).

Drills may be held to teach staff how to diagnose and respond to various accidents, but this may not have much utility. The events are rare and unpredictable, and any skills or knowledge acquired are likely to be lost through disuse or are only partially applicable to the malfunction at hand (Reason 1990, 183).

We need to learn from technological problems and try our best to invest in better equipment that present less chance for failure. If failure occurs, however, a fail-safe system should be in place that limits the damage.

REFERENCES

Bogner, M. S. 1994. "Human Error in Medicine: A Frontier for Change." In *Human Error in Medicine*, edited by M. S. Bogner, 377–78. Hillsdale, NJ: Lawrence Erlbaum Associates.

Casey, S. 1993. *Set Phasers on Stun and Other True Tales of Design, Technology, and Human Error.* Santa Barbara, CA: Aegean Publishing Co.

Chiles, J. R. 2001. *Inviting Disaster: Lessons from the Edge of Technology.* New York: Harper Business.

Hayward, R. A., and T. P. Hofer. 2001. "Estimating Deaths Due to Medical Errors." *Journal of the American Medical Association* 286 (4): 415–20.

Joint Commission on Accreditation of Healthcare Organizations (JCAHO). 2003. [Online information; retrieved 12/03.] http://www.jcaho.org/news + room/news + release + archives /wss_news_release_1202.htm.

Kohn, L. T., J. Corrigan, and M. S. Donaldson (eds.). 2000. *To Err Is Human: Building a Safer Health System*. Washington, DC: National Academy Press.

Moray, N. 1994. "Error Reduction as a Systems Problem." In *Human Error in Medicine*, edited by M. S. Bogner, 67–91. Hillsdale, NJ: Lawrence Erlbaum Associates.

Perrow, C. 1999. *Normal Accidents: Living with High-Risk Technologies*, 72–89; 89–100. Princeton, NJ: Princeton University Press.

Reason, J. 1990. *Human Error*. Cambridge, England: Cambridge University Press.

———. 1997. *Managing the Risks of Organizational Accidents*. Burlington, VT: Ashgate Publishing Co.

Richardson, W. C., and J. M. Corrigan. 2003. "Provider Responsibility and System Redesign: Two Sides of the Same Coin." *Health Affairs* 22 (2): 116–18.

Spath, P. L. (ed.). 2000. *Error Reduction in Health Care: A Systems Approach to Improving Patient Safety*. San Francisco: Jossey-Bass.

Vincent, C., G. Neale, and M. Woloshynowych. 2001. "Adverse Events in British Hospitals: Preliminary Retrospective Record Review." *British Medical Journal* 322 (7285): 517-19.

Weick, K. 2002. "Reduction of Medical Errors Through Mindful Interdependence." In *Medical Error: What Do We Know? What Do We Do?* edited by M. M. Rosenthal and K. M. Sutcliffe, 177–78. San Francisco: Jossey-Bass.

CHAPTER 2

Leadership

Role

> Leadership is liberating people to do what is required of them in the most effective and humane way possible (DePree 1989, 1).

The road to a safer organization begins with understanding the current environment in terms of both physician and employee attitudes and the organization's way of caring for its patients. This is a difficult journey for healthcare leaders to take, but it is necessary to regain the trust of patients and communities. Leaders owe the people in their institutions a clear statement of the organization's values and a "new reference point for what caring, purposeful, committed people can be in the institutional setting" (DePree 1989).

Why is organizational change so difficult and innovation so lacking in hospitals, especially with respect to responding to the problem of medical error? ▶

In this chapter, a number of explanations are presented. All of them begin and end with leadership.

LEADERSHIP STRUCTURE OF U.S. HOSPITALS

The control of hospitals by physicians began to wane in the late 1930s and 1940s, when lay administrators became more common. Over time, three separate lines of authority evolved in hospitals: the board of trustees, the medical staff, and administration. This runs contrary to a sociologist's view of a bureaucracy with one clear line of control. Instead, hospitals remain "incompletely integrated, both as organizations and as a system of organizations—a case of blocked institutional development, a precapitalist institution radically changed in its functions and moral identity but only partially transformed in its organizational structure" (Starr 1982).

Leadership Changes

Substantial turnover in administrative leadership continues—approximately 14 percent of healthcare CEOs move on every year. Such frequent changes in leadership may result in an inconsistent focus, a shift in priorities and initiatives, and failure to develop stable and trusting relationships with physicians and staff. Other executive and managerial positions may turn over even more frequently and aggravate such problems.

Gap in Clinical Knowledge

The "product" of the healthcare industry is a patient transformed (in the broadest terms) from illness to health. In many other businesses, the CEO and members of the administrative staff have grown up with the industry and understand it from the ground up. This is not so in healthcare, where most of the leaders have no direct experience with the business product.

The clinical knowledge deficit of lay leadership is impossible to correct except at the most rudimentary level. Health professionals, on the other hand, are able to enter administrative positions, acquiring additional education through formal business training or other intensive programs.

Delegation of Quality Oversight to Medical Staff

As a result of the clinical knowledge gap, boards of trustees have delegated the oversight of the quality of clinical care to the medical staff. Medical staff leaders are responsible for ensuring that physicians are practicing quality medicine and that deviations from appropriate care or the occurrence of untoward events are systematically and thoroughly evaluated.

Physicians scrupulously protect the nature of their deliberations and the scope of their peer review and clinical departmental activities. The board is likely to receive information on these activities only in summary formats or through risk management reports.

This practice of quality delegation is a serious and long-standing deficiency in hospitals. It retards an aggressive pursuit of the causes of adverse events and limits the development of systems to prevent error and to ensure a consistently high standard of patient care.

CULTURES OF THE HEALTH PROFESSIONS

Physician View of Error

Physician errors can be explained through the following categories (Bosk 1981):

- *Technical errors* occur when a physician's skills are not up to the task he or she is trying to perform.

Physicians expect such errors from every doctor, because medicine is an imperfectly applied discipline. In fact, they often view these incidents as positive learning experiences, even though a patient may have been injured. Technical errors are more common among younger physicians and are usually not damaging to their reputation.

- *Judgmental errors* occur when a physician selects incorrect treatment plans. Physicians are often not criticized for judgmental errors because of their past successes and reputation as well as their colleagues' reluctance to peer through the "retrospectoscope," where vision is always 20/20.

- *Normative errors* result from a physician's failure to discharge his or her obligations in a conscientious manner. Physicians who commit such errors may be immune to criticisms for at least two reasons. First, a physician is presumed to be of high moral stature because of his or her board certification, state licensure, membership in professional societies, or appointment to the medical staff. Second, a physician does not work under an authority figure who can accuse him or her of such an error.

- *Significant uncertainty errors* are made in areas of medicine where no objective rules or standards are available. This leads physicians to rely on their training and experiences or on literature that supports their particular protocol or treatment plan. Physicians who review untoward outcomes of such errors are hesitant to be critical because of the lack of standards.

Physicians may place greater weight on adherence to normative or ethical behavior than on technical and judgmental actions. Their rationale seems to be that moral rectitude and conforming to professional standards are easier to judge than the mechanics of medical practice. The medical profession needs to balance its excessive focus on individual control with a greater sense of corporate responsibility (Bosk 1981).

How Health Professionals Deal with Error

Healthcare leaders must understand the manner in which health professionals view and deal with error. As Leape (2001) stated, "While many other human enterprises, such as aviation, building, and military operations, are associated with substantial hazard, in no other situation is the harm and suffering caused by the action of individuals whose sole purpose is to relieve suffering and in whom the victim places a profound and personal trust—doctors and nurses.... [T]his very personal sense of affront and betrayal that accounts for the intense emotion surrounding medical injury, particularly when caused by error."

The cultures of physicians and nurses emphasize precision, high standards of performance, and a strong sense of personal responsibility (Jones 2002). Fundamentally, health professionals do not take kindly to error, except with respect to its educational value in the training environment. Therefore, encouraging both an open dialog about error and an approach that emphasizes the systems nature of most adverse outcomes is not a simple task.

Healthcare leaders must commit to the task of reducing medical error by setting it as an organizational priority, but such an effort is insufficient unless it becomes part of the organizational fabric.

According to Max DePree (1989), leaders must "liberate" people to do the right thing, utilizing their own skills and talents. In this view, every member of an organization has an opportunity to show leadership.

One person leading the pursuit of patient safety is a fruitless task. Organizations must learn to leverage their workforce so that hundreds and thousands pairs of eyes are searching for errors and so that everyone feels comfortable identifying and reporting safety issues.

LACK OF AWARENESS

We watch leaders of the tobacco, automobile, and accounting industries sit before congressional hearings to get to the root of their problems. How would healthcare executives fare under such questioning? Would they deny knowledge of their hospital's incidence of wound infection or of the percentage of their patients with acute myocardial infarction discharged without recommended drugs? Can they respond to questions about how well they are doing at eliminating medical error and adverse outcomes?

If leaders are not knowledgeable about the details of the patient care provided and the outcomes of that care, they cannot begin the journey to improvement of quality and elimination of adverse outcomes. Therefore, the first thing they need to understand is that ignorance is not an option.

Being aware of the results of patient care processes requires consistent and comprehensive analysis of processes and outcomes and a well-developed communication plan. This entails allocation of significant resources to ensure that data are collected and that information is generated and reported in a timely fashion. The organization must develop a philosophy of not only addressing errors when they occur but also of looking for means to improve processes to prevent mistakes from happening in the first place.

NARROW FOCUS

Healthcare executives and boards are most comfortable dealing with the organization's finances because they are easily measured and do not require much interpretation, unlike clinical processes. However, just because something is easily measured does not mean it is what one should be measuring. An inordinate focus on financial performance sends this clear message to everyone in the organization: This is what is meaningful. Financial success is, however, only a byproduct of excellent patient care, which is where the emphasis should be.

When leaders and industries put corporate profits before public safety, the results are disastrous. For years, General Motors (GM) knew that the gas tank in its automobiles needed to be in a protected position to prevent it from rupturing and catching fire in the event of a rear-end collision. Despite that information, GM placed the gas tank in its 1979 Chevy Malibu a mere 11 inches from the rear of the car. In a later lawsuit, a Los Angeles jury awarded $4.9 billion to 6 people who were severely burned when the gas tank in their Malibu exploded following an accident. The verdict was no doubt influenced by the finding that GM would have had to pay only $8.59 to relocate the gas tank (Personal Injury Law Page 2003). More recently, Ford and Bridgestone/Firestone were castigated for their failure to address faulty tires that led to multiple deaths in both Europe and the United States. Although these companies had information that their product was inferior, they elected to keep silent and thus caused unnecessary loss of life. At the congressional hearings on the tire recall, Senator John McCain (2000) stated, "When manufacturers fail to tell the truth or purposely neglect to report safety data, and people lose their lives, severe penalties must result."

DIFFERENCE BETWEEN PERCEPTION AND REALITY

Michael Millenson (2003), in a *Health Affairs* article, indicts physicians and hospitals for their failure to act more aggressively to prevent medical error despite overwhelming evidence of the problem. A 1978 *Western Journal of Medicine* article determined from California medical records that 140,000 treatment-caused injuries, including almost 14,000 fatalities, occurred. Using that year as a starting point of when the healthcare profession was first informed of the price of medical error, Millenson suggests that about 1 to 2.5 million people died from treatment in U.S. hospitals between 1978 and 1999, when the IOM report was published. This amounts to an average of 9 to 22 deaths a year at each of the 5,500 acute care hospitals in the country. When numbers like this are reported in the media, the public has a right to question what is being done to reduce such loss of life.

Deaths from adverse events do not occur like those from airline disasters, which may kill several hundred people at one time. A hospital may have only a small number of such deaths each month. As a result, when physicians and leaders look at their hospital's mortality rate, they do not see the catastrophes. The one or two obvious cases may get attributed to bad luck rather than to bad systems. Cases that do involve medical error may not get the broad exposure or the detailed investigation that could pinpoint a systemic malfunction.

A traditional blaming culture keeps such adverse outcomes from becoming common knowledge. Such outcomes can be attributed to an incompetent physician, nurse, or other healthcare worker, and that individual can be disciplined or terminated to take care of the problem.

A catastrophe can mobilize people to act, but the subtle or insidious causes of such an event demand more from healthcare organizations. What is required is leadership and a culture that seeks the reasons for unexpected and subpar outcomes and that does not tolerate mediocrity. This is what Dr. Codman had in mind when he developed the end-results system (see Sidebar D). Organizations must measure the outcomes of diagnosis and treatment and seek to improve them so that deficiencies are identified before they cause serious injury or death.

This is hard and risky work that entails confronting and changing established professional norms and installing a new culture of accountability.

COMPLEXITY OF THE HEALTHCARE EXECUTIVE'S JOB

The healthcare executive's job is incredibly complex, and healthcare is one of the most difficult businesses to manage for a number of reasons:

1. Patients assume they are receiving a quality product and, in most cases, expect nothing less than perfection.
2. Hospitals purchase the latest technology; hire and train the best staff; and keep the facility up-to-date and open 24 hours a day, 365 days a year—all while receiving either a fixed reimbursement or a substantial discount off charges.
3. Patient care is directed by a group of professionals who generates the majority of costs but over which the executive has little influence.

4. The topic of adverse outcomes and patient safety challenges healthcare executives to leave their comfort zone and confront the status quo. An executive must now prove to be knowledgeable about patient outcomes and must be committed to their improvement.

ERA OF PUBLIC REPORTING AND ACCOUNTABILITY

The call for public accountability is beginning to suggest a new reality for America's healthcare institutions—a reality in which these organizations' accomplishments and failures will be matters of public record. A number of quality ratings are published each year, but these have focused only on the so-called "best" in American healthcare, including the "100 Best Hospitals" and a city's or region's "Best Doctors."

Most of these lists include little data on outcomes of care. Rather, they are usually heavily reliant on measurable financial parameters, established "centers of excellence," or reputation. Some Internet sites have gone further however, abstracting data from Medicare files to rank hospitals based on their mortality and complication rates for certain diseases or procedures.

All the complexities of the patient care process are distilled into some simplistic rating system for the consumer's review. The methodology by which such ratings are constructed is generally not discussed by such agencies, and there is no guarantee that a hospital that rates highly in one area provides equally good care in others. See Sidebar E.

The leader's roles in this era of public accountability are as follows:

- Understand the goals and objectives of the various constituencies who advocate for a greater transparency for healthcare outcomes.
- Ensure that the organization is meeting benchmarks for certain reported outcomes or has programs in place to move in that direction.
- Voluntarily participate in outcomes initiatives sponsored by federal, state, and regulatory agencies as well as other credible organizations committed to patient safety and quality of care. Participation can give needed impetus to an organization's quality improvement program and can encourage collaboration among all stakeholders.

SIDEBAR E

Presentations of outcomes information in an incomplete manner have many troubling aspects. Two in particular need to be confronted by healthcare leaders:

1. If reported outcomes fall under the established standards, should leaders be actively involved in improving them? If not, why not?
2. Should leaders once again allow non-healthcare agencies to force them into a reactive posture?

If healthcare institutions do not take a more aggressive posture, many of these non-healthcare organizations are likely to supplant them in advancing the agenda of quality and patient safety.

Governmental Safety Initiatives

In 2000, the U.S. Department of Health and Human Services (HHS) developed the Patient Safety Task Force to coordinate all intergovernmental activities related to the collection of patient safety data. HHS also now reports on the quality of nursing homes and home care agencies (CMS 2003; Clancy and Scully 2003).

In 2001, the Agency for Healthcare Research and Quality (AHRQ) distributed a document, entitled "Making Healthcare Safer," that lists 73 interventions that are likely to improve patient safety. From the 73 items, AHRQ identified 11 that are proven to be highly effective but that are not routinely employed by practitioners (see Table 1) (Shojania et al. 2001). AHRQ also developed a web-based, peer-reviewed medical journal that presents medical error cases for discussion and in-depth analysis.

These two governmental initiatives represent an excellent starting point for healthcare executives to audit their own institutional practices and to engage physicians in evidence-based improvement efforts.

National Quality Forum

The National Quality Forum (NQF 2002) is a private, not-for-profit organization whose mission is to improve American healthcare through endorsement of consensus-based national standards for measurement and public reporting of healthcare performance data (Quality Forum 2003). The NQF completed a report, entitled "Serious Reportable Events in

Table 2. NQF's List of Serious Reportable Events

Surgical Events
- Surgery performed on the wrong body part
- Surgery performed on the wrong patient
- Wrong surgical procedure performed on a patient
- Retention of a foreign object in a patient after surgery or other procedure
- Intraoperative or immediately postoperative death in an ASA Class I patient

Procedure or Device Events
- Patient death or serious disability associated with the use of contaminated drugs, devices, or biologics provided by the healthcare facility
- Patient death or serious disability associated with the use or function of a device in patient care in which the device is used or functions other than as intended
- Patient death or serious disability associated with intravascular air embolism that occurs while being cared for in a healthcare facility

Patient Protection Events
- Infant discharged to the wrong person
- Patient death or serious disability associated with patient elopement (disappearance) for more than four hours
- Patient suicide, or attempted suicide resulting in serious disability, while being cared for in a healthcare facility

Care Management Events
- Patient death or serious disability associated with a medication error (e.g., errors involving the wrong drug, wrong dose, wrong patient, wrong time, wrong rate, wrong preparation, or wrong route of administration)
- Patient death or serious disability associated with a hemolytic reaction due to the administration of ABO-incompatible blood or blood products
- Maternal death or serious disability associated with labor or delivery in a low-risk pregnancy while being cared for in a healthcare facility
- Patient death or serious disability associated with hypoglycemia, the onset of which occurs while the patient is being cared for in a healthcare facility
- Stage 3 or 4 pressure ulcers acquired after admission to a healthcare facility
- Patient death or serious disability due to spinal manipulative therapy

Environmental Events
- Patient death or serious disability associated with an electric shock while being cared for in a healthcare facility
- Any incident in which a line designated for oxygen or other gas to be delivered to a patient contains the wrong gas or is contaminated by toxic substances
- Patient death or serious disability associated with a burn incurred from any source while being cared for in a healthcare facility
- Patient death associated with a fall while being cared for in a healthcare facility
- Patient death or serious disability associated with the use of restraints or bedrails while being cared for in a healthcare facility

Criminal Events
- Any instance of care ordered or provided by someone impersonating a physician, nurse, pharmacist, or other licensed healthcare provider
- Abduction of a patient at any age
- Sexual assault on a patient within or on the grounds of a healthcare facility
- Death or significant injury of a patient or staff member resulting from a physical assault (i.e., battery) that occurs within or on the grounds of a healthcare facility

In January 2004, the Centers for Medicare & Medicaid Services (CMS 2003) announced that hospitals that do not submit performance data for the following measures will receive 0.4 percent smaller Medicare payments in fiscal year 2005:

1. *Measures for acute myocardial infarction*: aspirin at arrival and on discharge, beta-blocker at arrival and on discharge, ACE (angiotensin converting enzyme) inhibitor for LVSD (left ventricular systolic dysfunction).
2. *Measures for diagnosis of heart failure*: left ventricular assessment, ACE inhibitor for LVSD.
3. *Measures for diagnosis of pneumonia*: timing of antibiotic administration, pneumococcal vaccination, oxygen assessment

Healthcare," with the goal of forming the basis for a national, state-based event-reporting system that could lead to substantial improvements in the quality of patient care. See Table 2.

The National Voluntary Hospital Reporting Initiative

In December 2002, the American Hospital Association, the Federation of American Hospitals, and the Association of American Medical Colleges formed this voluntary initiative to collect and report hospital quality-performance information.

This effort intends to make crucial information about hospital performance available to the public and to stimulate and support efforts to improve quality. Voluntary reporting is an important first step to achieve this goal. See Sidebar F.

The future direction of public reporting will be guided by the following:

1. Institute of Medicine's 20 priority areas for quality improvement (see Table 3),
2. National Quality Forum's accountability initiatives, and
3. Institute of Medicine's six aims for an ideal healthcare system (see Table 4 on the following page).

The Impact of Public Reporting

The impact of public reporting is illustrated by the results of a project in Wisconsin. Alliance, a large employer-purchasing cooperative, produced and distributed a report on hospital safety that involved 24 hospitals in south central Wisconsin. The report appeared in the newspaper and on the Internet. Copies were mailed to employees' homes and distributed by

Table 3. IOM's 20 Key Areas in Transforming the Healthcare System
1. Asthma
2. Care coordination
3. Children with special healthcare needs
4. Diabetes
5. End of life with advanced organ system failure
6. Evidence-based cancer screening
7. Frailty associated with old age
8. Hypertension
9. Immunization
10. Ischemic heart disease
11. Major depression
12. Medication management
13. Nosocomial infections
14. Obesity
15. Pain control in advanced cancer
16. Pregnancy and childbirth
17. Self-management/health literacy
18. Severe and persistent mental illness
19. Stroke
20. Tobacco-dependence treatment in adults

community groups and libraries. The study included 98 other hospitals in Wisconsin that either received a private copy of their report or no copy.

Approximately nine months after the report's distribution, all participating hospitals were surveyed regarding their ongoing quality improvement efforts. The public-report hospitals reported a significantly higher number of improvement efforts in obstetrics and cardiac care than did the private-report and no-report hospitals (Hibbard, Stockard, and Tusler 2003).

This project indicates that public reporting exerts the type of pressure that was envisioned by Alliance. Such positive results are only likely to encourage further efforts around the country.

PERCEIVED LACK OF A BUSINESS CASE FOR QUALITY

One of the reasons that providers have not more vigorously pursued quality improvements is their perceived lack of a business case for such efforts. Until an economic analysis indicates a demand for quality, providers have no incentive to invest in quality improvements. Such

Table 4. IOM's Six Aims for an Ideal Healthcare System
1. Healthcare should be safe.
2. Healthcare should be effective.
3. Healthcare should be patient-centered.
4. Healthcare should be timely.
5. The healthcare system should be efficient.
6. Healthcare should be equitable.

investment should result in a return in the form of increased reimbursement, decreased losses, avoidance of cost, or improved organizational functioning and stability.

According to Leatherman and colleagues (2003), a number of obstacles impede healthcare organizations from making this investment:

- The payment system does not discriminate between high-quality and poor-quality care. Payment is the same regardless of care outcomes.
- Patients are not readily able to perceive quality-of-care differences. This may change as more information becomes available, as consumers become better educated, and if employer coalitions are successful at directing patients to higher-quality facilities.

The CMS–Premier, Inc. (CMS 2003) project is organized as follows:

- Financial bonuses to hospitals are based on specific quality measures for certain clinical conditions—heart attack, heart failure, hip and knee replacements, pneumonia, and coronary artery bypass grafts.
- Proposed measures are derived from the Leapfrog Group, AHRQ patient safety indicators, Core Measures of JCAHO, CMS's 7th Scope of Work, NQF indicators, and the National Voluntary Hospital Reporting Initiative.
- Hospitals in the top 20 percent for quality receive a bonus.
- Hospitals in the top decile for a given diagnosis receive a 2 percent bonus of their Medicare payments for the condition.
- Hospitals in the second decile receive a 1 percent bonus.
- Hospitals participating in the project receive previously collected quality data from the Premier Perspective database as a historical reference.

Results of the project's first year should be reported on the CMS web site in early 2005. The report will recognize those hospitals that achieved the highest quality and those that received bonuses.

Paying for Quality

In 2003, CMS began a project that would, in fact, reimburse hospitals at a higher rate if they can show evidence of quality outcomes in a number of acute care areas. CMS's partner in this effort is Premier, Inc., a nationwide organization of not-for-profit hospitals that could track and report quality data for 34 measures at its member hospitals. See Sidebar G.

The Leapfrog Group Standards

The Leapfrog Group is sponsored by the Business Roundtable, a national association of *Fortune* 500 CEOs. This voluntary program mobilizes large purchasers to alert the healthcare industry about the major improvements in patient safety and customer value that need to be recognized and rewarded with preferential use and other intensified market reinforcements.

The Leapfrog Group aims to enhance the dialog among healthcare purchasers, providers, and consumers. It also seeks to significantly influence the efforts to address the yearly death toll from preventable medical mistakes.

The Leapfrog Group has identified three safety measures or standards that inform comparisons of healthcare provider performance, recognition, and reward:

- A payment structure does not exist that rewards investment in programs that benefit patients years into the future (e.g., smoking cessation, diabetes management).
- Patients do not have the option of purchasing more customized healthcare benefits that focus on quality or better chronic-disease management.
- Many proven quality interventions are not routinely employed because information about them is not easily available or is not well appreciated by providers. This may require more investment in improved clinical information and decision support systems.

1. *Computerized physician order entry (CPOE).* This has been shown to significantly reduce serious prescribing errors in hospitals.
2. *Evidence-based hospital referral.* Referring patients who need certain complex medical procedures to hospitals that offer the best survival based on scientifically valid criteria can reduce mortality risk by more than 30 percent.
3. *Intensive care unit (ICU) physician staffing.* If ICUs are staffed 24 hours a day by physicians trained in critical care medicine, the death rate of ICU patients can be reduced by more than 10 percent.

These standards apply to urban and suburban hospitals only; rural hospitals have been excluded (The Leapfrog Group 2003). Hospitals are asked to voluntarily complete the Leapfrog Survey, which includes questions about compliance or plans to comply with the recommendations. The results of the survey as of late 2003 are as follows:

- Less than 4 percent of responding hospitals had CPOE.
- Only 19 percent had fully implemented ICU staffing.
- The volume criteria for certain procedures were fulfilled by between 12 percent and 15.6 percent of responding hospitals. The lowest percentage was for coronary artery bypass surgery and the highest was for abdominal aortic aneurysm repair.

Problems with the Standards

Adhering to these three standards is difficult because of the following reasons:

- CPOE is expensive and has sustained a number of highly publicized failures that are primarily related to physician resistance (Ornstein 2003). *Modern Healthcare*'s annual information technology survey revealed that healthcare executives were less inclined to implement CPOE in 2004 than in 2003 (Morrisey 2004).
- Only a few studies quantify the impact of CPOE on drug errors. The major institutions that are reporting success are Brigham and Women's Hospital in Boston and LDS in Salt Lake City (Mello, Studdert, and Brennan 2003).
- Physician staffing for ICUs is problematic given the relative shortage of trained intensivists.
- Implementing volume criteria dramatically changes referral patterns and causes patients to

The reasonableness standard may be applied in three areas (Mello, Studdert, and Brennan 2003):

1. *Technology.* Hospitals that are slow in adopting new technology that is clearly beneficial to patients may face legal consequences. Some courts use a crude formula: compare the burden of acquiring the technology against the probability of injury without the technology, then multiply that by the severity of the injury. If the burden of acquiring the technology is less than the probability, the hospital may be found liable.

2. *Practice guidelines.* Although clinical practice guidelines are still not used by a majority of physicians, they can still be a persuasive argument that a provider has not met the reasonableness standard, especially if the guidelines are regarded as authoritative within the medical community.

3. *Informed consent.* A physician who practices at a hospital that offers no 24-hour ICU coverage by intensivists may need to inform his or her patients that their outcomes would be better if they are transferred to an institution that has such a capability. Failure to do so may lead the patient to sue the physician for inadequate informed consent and the hospital for not implementing the standard.

travel well outside of their communities for care.

In addition, the Leapfrog standards can complicate the malpractice picture for hospitals. Medical malpractice is a matter of state law. State court judges define the legal standard of care, and this may lead to variability from state to state. In the past, judges have usually defined negligence as a failure to adhere to a standard of care that would ordinarily be expected of a physician in the same specialty practicing in the same community. Over the last few years, however, a number of states have adopted a *reasonableness standard*. This standard, in some cases, has led to providers being deemed negligent even though they did not depart from the usual standard of care. See Sidebar H.

Malpractice cases that reference Leapfrog standards must be watched closely. They can affect how quickly some of these standards are adopted by hospitals.

These criteria put forth by business leaders may seem arbitrary, and complying with them may be problematic. However, until healthcare leaders offer credible alternatives by which to measure quality, the Leapfrog Group standards will continue to have an impact.

DIFFICULTY OF ASSESSING PHYSICIAN COMPETENCE

With all this demand for public accountability of hospitals, a call to assess physician competence may be in order as well. However, barriers to such an endeavor exist:

- Most medical specialties lack a comprehensive set of evidence-based measures either for outcomes of care or for processes linked to improved patient outcomes.

- Outside of a few general measures, such as mortality and infection rates, there are no thresholds for less-than-perfect performance and no agreement on the tolerance for deviation from existing thresholds.
- Physicians may not have adequate numbers of patients with a particular condition to conform to a sample size on which statistical measures can be performed with confidence.
- Patients are not randomly allocated to physicians, and systematic differences likely exist between physicians and their patient populations.
- Risk-adjustment methodologies are costly and difficult to validate.
- Attempts to define a physician's competence on the basis of his or her performance on a small number of clinical indicators may run the risk of misrepresenting a physician's competence in performing the rest of his or her duties.
- Measures employed to evaluate physicians must be feasible to collect and reasonable in cost.
- Measures of functional status and long-term outcomes can be difficult

and expensive to obtain. But they are of great benefit in evaluating orthopedists, rheumatologists, and ophthalmologists, for example.

For all the above reasons, physician clinical-performance assessment may not be accomplished in any comprehensive way at present (Landon et al. 2003).

THE POTENTIAL FOR CONFLICT OVER OUTCOMES REPORTING

Hospitals are judged on clinical outcomes that result from the aggregate activities of their medical staffs. Quality of clinical care is where significant tension between healthcare executives and medical staff leaders is likely to develop.

The outcomes movement promises to be another battleground between healthcare executives and physicians. Public reporting of patient care outcomes will, of necessity, focus on hospitals. A hospital's accreditation, reimbursement, referrals, workforce and physician recruitment, charitable donations, and many other vital elements can be affected by the nature of such public data. Executives have no choice but to become more involved with clinical outcomes, which were heretofore the exclusive domain of the physician.

Physicians' Failure to Deliver Recommended Care

The quality of care provided to patients by American physicians is less than optimal. A study in the *New England Journal of Medicine* examines the frequency at which patients received recommended care for a number of acute and chronic conditions that represent the leading causes of illness, death, and utilization of healthcare. Through both telephone interviews and chart reviews, the researchers found that only 54.9 percent of study participants received recommended care, while 53.5 of the patients received recommended acute care (McGlynn et al. 2003).

Medical Staff's Responsibility

Medical staffs are supposed to oversee clinical quality through appropriate credentialing and recredentialing of its physicians and through ongoing peer review of its members. The results of such activities, and the lists of physicians recommended for appointment or reappointment, are given to the board for action. In addition, medical staffs are responsible for identifying the areas of care delivery that would benefit from improvement and for developing plans to decrease patient morbidity and mortality.

How well are medical staffs performing this delegated function, and what is their opinion about their responsibility for quality of care?

VHA Inc. (2002) conducted a survey of over 500 physicians in late 2001 and early 2002 to determine whether medical staff organizations are interested, competent, and have the resources to oversee meaningful improvements in the quality of clinical care. Only 19 percent of surveyed physicians felt that ensuring quality and patient satisfaction were the primary responsibility of the medical staff organization. Thirty-four percent felt that this responsibility rested with the healthcare organization. Neither chief medical officers nor physicians saw clinical excellence as the most valuable role for the medical staff organization. In addition, the survey revealed that physician attitudes toward national quality improvement and clinical improvement programs were quite conservative.

Healthcare leaders can use a number of remedies to address this conflict.

EMPLOY A MORE AGGRESSIVE APPROACH
Organizations can aggressively take on the oversight of clinical quality by hiring chief medical officers, running the medical staff office, and ensuring that enough qualified staff are available to operationalize performance improvement efforts.

Most physicians now spend little time at the hospital, doing the bulk of their work in the ambulatory environment. In addition, many physicians in urban and suburban markets are members of multiple medical staffs, which explains why the organized medical staff finds it difficult to carry out its delegated role for quality oversight. Although physicians are concerned about the quality of care that each of their patients receive, they are generally disinterested in hospital quality initiatives and feel that the national effort to promote quality care overstates the problem and will not be beneficial (VHA 2002). Therefore, left to their own devices, medical staffs are not likely to mount any significant quality improvement efforts.

RESTRUCTURE RELATIONSHIPS Hospitals must be diligent in determining who is appointed to their medical staffs; must ensure that practitioners are up-to-date in their practices; and must supervise all care rendered within the organization, including services provided by physicians.

Marren and his colleagues (2003) suggest the structural silos (medical staff and management) that exist within the modern hospital are impediments to achieving quality care. The emphasis by physicians on self-governance, self-monitoring, and self-discipline creates a substantial obstacle to an organization's goal to be a safe, effective, and efficient system. This isolation of the medical staff negates the reality that the delivery of care is a multidisciplinary process and must be approached as such. Each board needs to ensure that its bylaws specifically detail the responsibilities it delegates to the medical staff and the consequences of not accomplishing these tasks. In short, the governing body must take a greater role in ensuring that quality and safety goals are accomplished and continuously improved by remaining involved in all aspects of clinical operations despite delegating certain of these responsibilities (Marren, Feazell, and Paddock 2003).

EMPHASIZE THE NEED FOR ADAPTIVE CHANGE The relationship between the board, executives, and medical staff must be changed to enable the organization to reduce medical errors and to improve clinical outcomes. Leaders are often approached to provide solutions to organizational problems. Solutions, however, must arise from those directly involved with the problem. This type of learning necessitates that people change their attitudes, values, and behaviors; the greater the change required, the greater the resistance (Heifetz and Linsky 2002). In seeking greater involvement in the issue of quality, boards and healthcare executives are sure to encounter substantial resistance from physicians, who may interpret such actions as an attempt to limit their autonomy. As noted by Pont (2000):

> Economic motivations alone, however, cannot justify the ardor of organized medicine's opposition to healthcare reform efforts throughout this century. It is my contention that physicians have been motivated primarily by a desire to protect their professional autonomy, viewing reform as a threat to this autonomy. They have consistently maintained this vigilant defense of their professional sphere even when

their political and economic interests would have dictated they act otherwise.

MAKE PATIENT SAFETY A PRIORITY An initiative to systematically improve outcomes and patient safety must be clearly articulated as an organizational priority by the governing body. The stimulus for an initiative may begin with the vision, dedication, and commitment of an individual. The success of the initiative, however, cannot depend on that one individual. In their book *Built to Last*, Collins and Porras (1994) relate this anecdote:

> Imagine you met a remarkable person who could look at the sun or stars at any time of the day or night and state the exact time and date.... This person would be an amazing time teller.... But wouldn't that person be even more amazing if instead of telling the time, he or she built a clock that could tell the time forever, even after he or she was gone?

The result of such an initiative must be a culture that values quality and abhors error. It cannot be dependent on the charisma of a board chair, CEO, or medical staff leader. Instead, the culture must persist in spite of changes in leadership. Pursuing a culture that values patient safety has an even greater ethical and moral dimension for leaders, which is outlined in Sidebar I.

CHANGE THE CULTURE Leaders can create an environment in which every member of a healthcare organization —from employees to physicians to healthcare executives and board members—feels a responsibility to protect patients and to ensure their well-being. Encouraging collaborative efforts so necessary to reducing error and improving quality allows individuals to contribute to solutions and taps their potential for creative thinking.

Error is part of human performance. Therefore, replacing a blaming culture with a just culture requires considerable organizational change. Such change is especially difficult in light of a tort system that seeks to identify the individuals responsible for less-than-optimal outcomes.

The American College of Physicians and the American Medical Association Council on Ethical and Judicial Affairs believe that in situations in which a patient suffers significant complications from a physician's error, the physician should inform the patient of all the facts necessary for understanding what transpired. The truth should be told, even when it is inconvenient or subjects one to personal risk (Smith and Forster 2000).

The value of developing such a collaborative, honest climate is that it liberates those concerned. For the parties involved, it eliminates the fear of being discovered and it allows them to seek forgiveness. It also encourages others to come together to support the individual and to seek solutions to prevent or minimize the recurrence of the mistake.

UNDERSTAND THE UNIVERSE OF OUTCOMES Most boards, executives, and physicians are unaware of where they stand in the universe of clinical outcomes because of the fragmented nature of data collection, the dearth of electronic medical records, and the lack of clinical information systems. They can only react to data found on the Internet, which are subject to truth or falsity.

Aggregating outcomes for various treatments and procedures; comparing the results to national standards, guidelines, or benchmarks; and bringing the organization and physicians into compliance are Herculean tasks. However, these may in fact be easier to do than dealing with isolated instances of medical error with bad outcomes. They may also be more important in the long run to the overall health of the community.

START WITH WHAT IS KNOWN Quality and safety efforts should begin with the basic finding from the literature: the American healthcare system is doing a poor job at providing recommended therapies. CMS's National Voluntary Hospital Reporting Initiative, with its ten parameters covering three conditions, is an excellent way to enlist physician support. Participation in this effort is voluntary, but it can yield significant advantage for the organization in its effort to improve patient care and minimize error. These parameters are data driven, endorsed by physicians and their societies, and have been shown to benefit patients. Achieving some small wins in this area allows the organization to tackle other, more substantial issues.

USE AN ASSESSMENT TOOL In 1995, two high-profile medication errors at the Dana-Farber Cancer Institute in Boston made national headlines. The event caused the organization to perform an in-depth examination of its culture and safety practices. Since then, Dana-Farber's chief operating officer, Jim Conway (2000), has been a highly visible advocate for patient safety. He crisscrosses the country to share the lessons he and his organization learned about preventing medical error. In addition, he developed a tool for healthcare executives (see Appendix A at the end of the book) that assesses leadership activities. It includes the following sections: personal education, call to action, practicing a culture of safety, and advancing the field. Completing all the elements of this tool requires substantial effort, considerable time, and a willingness to take risks by challenging the status quo. This tool should be the starting point for healthcare leaders who are seeking to minimize medical error and to develop a culture of safety.

A FINAL NOTE

Noted consultant Tom Atchison (2004) tells a story about a healthcare organization that was having significant difficulty in a number of critical areas. He met with its CEO and inquired how he could help. The CEO replied, "Tom, we need a new culture and I'd like it by next

Tuesday!" Organizations embarking on cultural change must be prepared for an intensive, long-term effort. Such a change may take 3 to 5 years and requires strong and sustained leadership.

In the last chapter, the development of a culture of safety is examined.

REFERENCES

Atchison, T. 2004. Personal communication, March.

Bosk, C. L. 1981. *Forgive and Remember: Managing Medical Failure*, 36–70; 168–72. Chicago: University of Chicago Press.

Centers for Medicare & Medicaid Services (CMS). 2003. [Online information; retrieved 12/03.] http://www.cms.hhs.gov and http://cms.hhs.gov/quality/hospital/PremierFactSheet.pdf.

Clancy, C. M., and T. Scully. 2003. "A Call to Excellence." *Health Affairs* 22 (2): 113–15.

Collins, J. C., and J. I. Porras. 1994. *Built to Last: Successful Habits of Visionary Companies*, 22–23. New York: Harper Business.

Conway, J. B. 2000. *Strategies for Leadership: Hospital Executives and Their Role in Patient Safety*. Chicago: American Hospital Association.

DePree, M. 1989. *Leadership Is an Art*, 11–22. New York: Dell.

Heifetz, R. A., and M. Linsky. 2002. *Leadership on the Line*, 13–14. Boston: Harvard Business School Press.

Hibbard, J. H., J. Stockard, and M. Tusler. 2003. "Does Publicizing Hospital Performance Stimulate Quality Improvement Efforts?" *Health Affairs* 22 (2): 84–94.

Jones, B. 2002. "Nurses and the 'Code of Silence'." In *Medical Error: What Do We Know? What Do We Do?* edited by M. M. Rosenthal and K. M. Sutcliffe, 86. San Francisco: Jossey-Bass.

Kouzes, J. M., and B. Z. Posner. 1995. *The Leadership Challenge: How to Keep Getting Extraordinary Things Done in Organizations*, 338. San Francisco: Jossey-Bass.

Landon, B. E., S. L. Norman, D. Blumenthal, and J. Daley. 2003. "Physician Clinical Performance Assessment." *Journal of the American Medical Association* 290 (9): 1183–89.

Leape, L. L. 2001. "Foreword: Preventing Medical Accidents: Is 'Systems Analysis' the Answer?" *American Journal of Law and Medicine* 27 (2-3): 145–48.

Leapfrog Group. 2003. [Online information; retrieved 12/03.] http://www.leapfroggroup.org/FactSheets/LF_FactSheet.pdf and http://www.leapfroggroup.org/Readout.pdf.

Leatherman, S., D. Berwick, D. Iles, L. S. Lewin, F. Davidoff, T. Nolan, and M. Bisognano. 2003. "The Business Case for Quality: Case Studies and an Analysis." *Health Affairs* 22 (2): 16–30.

Marren, J. P., G. L. Feazell, and M. W. Paddock. 2003. "The Hospital Board at Risk and the Need to Restructure the Relationship with the Medical Staff." *Annals of Health Law* 12 (2): 179–234.

McCain, J. 2000. "Statement of Chairman John McCain. Ford/Firestone Tire Recall Hearing. [Online information; retrieved 12/03.] http://commerce.senate.gov/hearings/0912mcc.pdf.

McGlynn E. A., S. M. Asch, J. Adams, J. Keesey, J. Hicks, A. DeCristofaro, and E. A. Kerr. 2003. "The Quality of Health Care Delivered to Adults in the United States." *New England Journal of Medicine* 348 (26): 2635–45.

Mello, M., D. M. Studdert, and T. A. Brennan. 2003. "The Leapfrog Standards: Ready to Jump from Marketplace to Courtroom?" *Health Affairs* 22 (2): 46–59.

Millenson, M. 2003. "The Silence." *Health Affairs* 22 (2): 103–12.

Morrisey, J. 2004. "Harmonic Divergence." *Modern Healthcare* 34 (8): 16.

National Quality Forum (NQF). 2002. "Serious Reportable Events in Healthcare: A National Quality Forum Consensus Report." Washington, DC: National Quality Forum.

Ornstein, C. 2003. "Hospital Heeds Doctors, Suspends Use of Software." *Los Angeles Times*, January 22, B1.

Personal Injury Law Page. 2003. [Online information; retrieved 12/03.] http://www .personalinjurylawpage.com/defective-products-transport/gastank-safety.htm.

Pont, E. A. 2000. "The Culture of Physician Autonomy: 1900 to the Present." *Cambridge Quarterly of Healthcare Ethics* 9 (1): 98–119.

Quality Forum. 2003. [Online information; retrieved 12/03.] http://www.qualityforum.org/mission /default.htm.

Sharpe, V. A., and A. I. Faden. 1998. *Medical Harm: Historical, Conceptual, and Ethical Dimensions of Iatrogenic Illness*, 29–31. Cambridge, England: Cambridge University Press.

Shojania, K. G., B. W. Duncan, K. M. McDonald, R. M. Wachter (eds.). 2001. *Making Health Care Safer: A Critical Analysis of Patient Safety Practices*. Evidence Report/Technology Assessment No. 43 (Prepared by the University of California at San Francisco-Stanford, Evidence-based Practice Center under Contract No. 290-97-0013). AHRQ Publication No. 01-E058, Rockville, MD: Agency for Healthcare Research and Quality.

Smith, M. L., and H. P. Forster. 2000. "Morally Managing Medical Mistakes." *Cambridge Quarterly of Healthcare Ethics* 9 (1): 38–53.

Starr, P. 1982. *The Social Transformation of American Medicine*, 178–79. New York: Basic Books, Inc.

VHA Inc. 2002. *Medical Staff Organizations: The Forgotten Covenant*. VHA Research Series, Volume 8. Irving, TX: VHA Inc.

CHAPTER 3

Culture of Safety

"Cultural traits and…practices detrimental to safety were allowed to develop, including reliance on past successes…" NASA (2003) about the Columbia Space Shuttle accident.

Preventable complications occur in small numbers every day at hospitals around the country. In aggregate, however, they represent a substantial problem, although they may not be as dramatic as the tragedies of the Tylenol (see Sidebar J) and Columbia Space Shuttle events.

Culture must be recognized as one of the essential building blocks in reconfiguring an organization to deal aggressively and forthrightly with adverse events. The healthcare industry has a long way to go in developing a culture that encourages the acknowledgment and open discussion of medical errors. Such an effort must begin with an organization's leadership—the board, administration, and medical staff. By example and by policy, these ▶

In September 1982, a young woman awoke with symptoms of a cold. Her parents gave her a Tylenol™ and sent her back to bed. She died later that day. Over the next 48 hours, six more people in the Chicago area died suddenly. Their main link: all had ingested Tylenol™ capsules that were tainted with over 60 milligrams of cyanide, a poison that is lethal at a dose a thousand times less. A media frenzy ensued, and people across the nation were alarmed.

At the time, Tylenol™ was one of Johnson & Johnson's most successful products, holding 37 percent of the over-the-counter pain-relief market. Advertising experts predicted that the scandal would ruin both Tylenol™ and Johnson & Johnson. But the company only focused on one thing: prevent any more harm to its customers. It stopped manufacturing and advertising the capsules, instructed the public to stop taking them, and recalled 31 million bottles.

Although the company knew that it was not responsible for the contamination, it forged ahead to ensure public safety. In explaining this course of action, company leaders pointed to the credo developed in 1940 by the company's founder, Robert Wood Johnson:

We believe our first responsibility is to the doctors, nurses, and patients, to mothers and fathers and all others who use our products and services. In meeting their needs everything we do must be of high quality... (Ethicon 2003).

Johnson & Johnson's response to the Tylenol™ scare has become a model for any business faced with a crisis—that is, customer safety first and company profits last (Kaplan 1998).

leaders must create an environment where safety is the top priority. This requires supporting the identification of systems failures, learning from mistakes, and making the necessary investments to improve performance.

Creating a culture of safety goes beyond senior leaders developing a set of policies and procedures. It means that the entire organization is guided by the belief that safety is important and that everyone is committed to upholding the established safety norms. If a top-down, bottoms-up approach is not embraced, little progress toward such a culture will be made.

This chapter presents the overarching elements of and the specific strategies for establishing a safety culture.

COMMITMENT

Foundational commitment needs to be made by the organization before it develops the structure that contributes to a safety culture. It requires an allocation of both human and financial resources, which are in short supply. Quality care costs money, and in the past no increases in reimbursement were given to organizations that showed improvement in patient outcomes. However, if organizations are serious about their mission, they will not make the trade-off that some industries have made between profitability and customer safety.

Sidebar K (see next page) provides an example of how an organization's commitment to a culture change promotes patient safety and quality.

TRUST

If trust exists between employees and senior management, introducing safety standards and norms to the organization is less difficult. In a trusting environment, employees feel supported when they report safety concerns and believe that doing so is part of their responsibility and contributes to improving patient care. They are confident that such reports are thoroughly analyzed, that appropriate actions are taken, and that feedback is provided to both the involved employees and the organization (Helmreich and Merritt 1998).

An organization will have a harder time with initiating a culture change if it is moving from a punitive culture in which errors were not reported or discussed for fear of retribution. Such a transformation requires longer-term work that involves ongoing dialog with physicians and employees. It also demands that senior leaders demonstrate their commitment to the values of a just safety culture and a learning organization.

Trust is the hardest value to earn and the easiest to lose. Trust cannot be banked. One untrustworthy act may destroy an individual's reputation as well as the fragile

structure of a developing safety culture.

ORGANIZATIONAL ASSESSMENT

A baseline assessment of the attitudes about safety of physicians, employees, executives, and board members is instructive. Such a survey can ask the following:

- What is your opinion about the frequency of serious errors in this hospital?
- Are errors freely reported?
- Is the culture punitive or supportive?

Information from this survey, allows a comparison between the old practice and the new model, after the latter is in place.

Following such a general survey, it is helpful to examine the organization in depth. Dr. Nancy Wilson (2000) of VHA developed a patient safety tool (see Appendix B at the end of the book) that asks organizations to evaluate the degree to which they have implemented a number of elements that support the development of a safety culture. This tool, along with the leadership assessment instrument (Appendix A) developed by Jim Conway and referred to in Chapter 2, provides an excellent method for evaluating any organization and its leaders seeking to improve patient outcomes and to reduce the incidence of medical error.

CORE BUSINESS

Ernest Codman said that the real product of a hospital is not its revenues but its success in treating its patients (Sharpe and Faden 1998). This means that the healthcare organization must critically evaluate both its focus and the areas in which its resources are being expended.

Physicians and nurses find it difficult to adjust to the fiscal realities that confront the organization and to embrace the need to be sensitive to resource expenditures. But they remain patient advocates, and as such they keep a close eye on whether the organization's actions are consistent with its words, asking, What is the first item on the agenda of management meetings? Is it about finances or patient care? Are clinical positions reduced or eliminated while the same number of executives, directors, and middle managers are maintained?

A safety environment requires a spiritual conversion of leaders. They must recommit to their core business of patient care and reorient all elements of their organizations to that end.

UNDERREPORTING

In healthcare, errors may be covered up by the unit or individuals responsible. This type of insularity is not helpful in building a safety culture. A process needs to be in place that allows safety concerns and reports of patient injuries or near misses to be reported to the organization's safety officer or risk manager without the reporter fearing retribution.

In 2001, JCAHO introduced new safety standards, including a requirement that hospitals disclose to patients any unanticipated outcomes of care, especially if the patient is harmed. An independent survey of risk managers at a nationally representative sample of 245 hospitals was conducted in 2002 to determine the extent of disclosure practices. About a third of the hospitals had disclosure policies, and 44 percent were in the process of developing such procedures. Over half said that they routinely informed patients and families when a patient had been injured as a result of their care. Sixty-five percent of hospitals responded that they always disclosed information in cases of death or serious injury. Only 37 percent stated they always disclosed when the outcome was serious but short term.

The Institute of Medicine's estimates of the most serious adverse events indicate that 44 to 66 medical injuries occur per 10,000 admissions. Only two of the hospitals in the survey were in this range, and less than 10 percent reported making more than 20 disclosures a year. This suggests that hospitals may not be identifying all of the serious injuries that occur as a result of medical care (Lamb et al. 2003).

The following factors may stimulate this underreporting:

- Hospitals may have a hard time identifying an adverse event because of the lack of definite criteria. There may be a question about whether the unfavorable outcome is related to treatment or the disease.
- A retrospective record review may be hampered by a chart that is incomplete, that is illegible, or that does not chronicle well the patient's course of treatment. In addition, all such chart reviews are highly dependent on the skill and attitude of the analyst.
- In healthcare, a bias is likely toward underdetection of adverse events. After all, it is difficult for practitioners to acknowledge that instead of helping a patient, they may have harmed the person.

Improved reporting is greatly aided by a more open and honest approach to the reality that errors do happen (Milstein and Adler 2003).

LESSONS FROM OTHER INDUSTRIES

Medicine has much to learn from other complex industries such as aviation and nuclear power, both of which have made major commitments to safety research and practice. These industries understand that even well-trained, well-meaning, and competent people make mistakes, which is particularly true when human beings interact with complex, evolving technology.

Complications of a significant error in these two industries can lead to the loss of hundreds or thousands of lives. Thus, these industries not only manage risk by preventing error, they also pay attention to avoiding consequences of errors that cannot be anticipated. They put a great deal of effort into creating cultures in which the reporting of errors and near misses is a strong organizational value. Employees understand that such reporting can save lives. This open communication is often rewarded and promotes the goal of organizational learning to improve. In addition, a great emphasis is placed on education, training, and teamwork (Wilson and Hatlie 2001).

To improve error reporting, a healthcare organization may consider establishing a hotline or a process similar to the Aviation Safety Reporting System (ASRS), which was developed in 1975 as a result of an agreement between the FAA (Federal Aviation Administration) and NASA (National Aeronautics and Space Administration). The ASRS works as follows (NASA 2003):

- Pilots, air traffic controllers, and others engaged in flight operations voluntarily submit reports when they observe or are involved in an incident in which safety is compromised.
- All reports are confidential and are de-identified before being entered into a database.
- Data are used to identify discrepancies and deficiencies in the National Aviation System (NAS), support improvements to the NAS, and strengthen human factors safety research.
- Guarantees and incentives are given for filing reports, and fines and penalties are waived for unintentional violations.
- A monthly safety bulletin is issued to more than 85,000 pilots, air traffic controllers, and others. It contains excerpts of incident reports with commentary as well as research summaries and related information.

COMMUNICATION AND COLLABORATION

Problems cannot be addressed if they are not known by people who are in a position to correct them. *Iceberg of ignorance* is a concept that suggests leaders know only 4 percent of an organization's problems. The frontline employees, however, know all of them (Healthcare Business Roundtable 2000).

One initiative that can help in making such important information more broadly known is to provide opportunities for all those involved in the delivery of care—nurses, physicians, executives, and other employees—to communicate about issues that directly affect patients (Bogner 1994). See Sidebar L for an example of such a collaborative activity.

ADVERSE OUTCOME ASSESSMENT

Organizations should determine the incidence of common adverse outcomes such as medication errors, falls, nosocomial infections, and surgical wound infections. The hospital's malpractice history may be instructive at uncovering potential

system problems. Errors of omission that can contribute to poor patient outcomes cannot be ignored, such as the timing of antibiotic administration in community-acquired pneumonia or the use of prophylactic antibiotics before surgery. The acquisition of such data is extremely important in mobilizing medical staff support for any improvement efforts.

A low number of adverse outcomes does not necessarily mean an organization is safe. Outcomes data can be an unreliable indicator, especially if the incidence of such events is low. There is a large random element in accident causation. This means that a "safe organization" can experience bad outcomes, and an "unsafe organization" may have a good track record for a long period.

Poor outcomes only show vulnerability. Regular assessments of organizational processes that are common to both quality and safety must be performed, and those in need of remediation must be identified (Reason 1997).

SAFETY SPACE

The concept of a *safety space* can be instructive (Reason 1997). The position an organization occupies (whether resistant or vulnerable to mistakes) is determined by the quality of the processes that are designed to defend against error. This position may change from time to time, especially in the presence of factors that cause the organization to become less concerned about safety.

Several factors allow an organization to maintain a high level of resistance against error (Reason 1997, 111):

- Commitment to a culture of safety. This includes not only organizational motivation but also appropriate allocation of resources (e.g., people, education, financial support, time).
- Technical competency. The organization must know what data to collect, how it should be interpreted, and to whom it should be disseminated.
- Recognition of the potential errors that threaten patient well-being.
- Realization that the journey to a safe environment never ends.

Effective safety management requires the use of both reactive and proactive measures. In any adverse outcome, appropriate resources must be available to isolate the root causes of the event and to define those aspects of the error that are within organizational control. It is important to understand the sequence of events leading to the accident, those that can be classified as active errors, and those that are the result of defects in the system of care (Feldman and Roblin 2000, 141).

CAUSES OF ERROR

When confronted by an error, people usually seize the most obvious cause. Such a limited analysis neglects other elements that may have contributed to the adverse outcome. Corrections of these elements, in the long run, have a greater impact on patient safety (Reason 1997). These include the strategic direction, goals, and objectives of the system in response to current environmental conditions and the assets allocated to achieve these ends.

Such decisions dictate the resources with which healthcare providers must operate and the constraints under which such resources are employed. For example, a decision to prohibit use of overtime and agency staff may have resulted in lower nurse-to-patient ratios. Decisions on capital equipment replacement or purchase may have compromised patient care. Reduced investment in training and education (which in healthcare is typically lower than in other major industries) may have led to personnel being less capable of dealing with problems. The deterioration of the physical plant can also be a contributing factor to adverse outcomes.

STRATEGIES FOR CREATING A SAFETY CULTURE

Sidebar M lists a number of specific interventions that can lessen the likelihood that individuals who provide care will make errors. This section offers strategies for developing a culture in which adverse outcomes are handled appropriately and in which safety is a priority for everyone.

Provide Safety Training

Educating the professional staff about patient safety should begin at new employee orientation and should focus on the organization's commitment to a safe environment. The employee handbook should include a statement about the organization's nonpunitive or just culture that encourages employees to identify and report medical errors and near misses. Hospital staff and physicians should receive regular, safety-related communication such as sentinel event alerts from JCAHO and updates on the organization's compliance to such recommendations. Organizations should emphasize successes as well as failures, noting what went right as well as what went wrong.

The use of simulators is increasing. Advances in technology, greater diagnostic and therapeutic options, and limited instruction time have increased their value. Simulation is helpful in the following ways (Issenberg et al. 1999):

- It provides laparascopic training to physicians without risking harm to patients.
- It creates a variety of scenarios to test anesthesiologist skills.
- It replicates a variety of cardiac conditions and multimedia computer systems, including patient-centered, case-based programs that can provide a generalist curriculum for cardiology.
- It addresses deficiencies in skills.
- It provides a mechanism for self-directed learning.

SIDEBAR M

Methods for Reducing Medical Errors

- Redesign error-prone processes or situations.
- Remove high concentrations of medications and solutions from the nursing unit to prevent inadvertent substitutions.
- Use sterile technique on insertion, antibiotic impregnated catheters, and chlorhexidine dressings to reduce central venous catheter infections.
- Check antibiotic and digoxin levels in the blood or measure certain coagulation parameters to identify an inappropriate medication dose (Spath 2000).

Minimize Reliance on Memory

Healthcare is a complex activity; therefore, it is unreasonable to expect a clinical caregiver to remember every aspect of every patient or every step in treating a disease. In an article, George Miller (1956) noted that "the span of immediate memory imposes severe limitations on the amount of information that we are able to receive, process, and remember." Memory can be further compromised by the frequent interruptions experienced by caregivers during their workday. Checklists, guidelines, standard protocols, clinical pathways, and computerized decision support tools can minimize reliance on memory.

Standardize Processes

Variability in healthcare is well documented. Patients with the same illness or disease are diagnosed, treated, and operated on in different ways by different practitioners.

In the operating room, for example, an orthopedist may select a hip prosthesis that another orthopedist may pass on, even though the type of prosthesis used may have shown no demonstrable difference in patient outcomes. The reason for the surgeon's choice may be something as simple as his or her familiarity with the prosthesis. This variation necessitates that the surgical assistant or scrub nurse learn the ins and outs of a number of devices and their tools, which increases the likelihood of errors as well as augments the cost of training.

Tasks should be standardized when possible, and variability should be eliminated when it has no benefit. Standard orders for common clinical conditions and procedures and standard protocols for medications can be helpful.

Move Toward Electronic Medical Records

Continuity of care depends on (1) the timely availability of records of a patient's previous illnesses or hospitalizations and (2) the format of those records that makes extraction of pertinent information possible. However, the medical record in a typical hospital is a nightmare. Crucial observations of physicians are mostly handwritten and are difficult to read. It is no wonder that medical errors caused by inadequate information exchange are frequent.

An electronic medical record is likely to be of inestimable benefit to patient care, enabling rapid transmission of complete patient data throughout the healthcare system.

Currently, more nurses are moving toward computerized documentation systems, while physicians still handwrite progress notes and patient care orders.

Improve Physician Communication

In June 2002, JCAHO issued a sentinel event alert that addresses patient death or permanent injury as a result of delays in treatment. Analysis of these cases reveals that the most common root cause of delays was a breakdown in communication (84 percent), which most often occurred with or between physicians (67 percent).

Some hospitals still allow a physician to request a consultation by a written order, leaving the nurse or unit clerk to call the consultant to pass on the request. In such cases, the reason that the consultation is being requested is often not specified, which may lead to an inordinate delay in urgent or emergent situations.

The medical staff should require physician-to-physician communication when consultations are requested. This will eliminate the likelihood of miscommunication and delay.

Manage the Staff Shortage

EDUCATE NEW HIRES The shortage of nurses and other health professionals places incredible demands on the existing workforce and has increased the likelihood of medical mistakes. Managers who are desperate for a "warm body" to staff their units may pay less attention to a new hire's experience, training, and capabilities. They may curtail orientation, and this may result in new nurses or technologists quickly finding themselves in over their heads when confronted by complex clinical situations. An adequate orientation is definitely a plus for employees.

When times get tough financially, educational initiatives are often the ones reduced or eliminated, aggravating the problems with inexperienced personnel. Education should be viewed as an investment that leads to greater efficiency, improved patient safety, reduced vacancies, and low turnover.

In addition, all new employees should be assigned a mentor for several reasons, including the following:

- It facilitates integration into the organization.
- It minimizes stress.
- It facilitates learning.
- It allows management to evaluate the new employee in real time and determine the individual's developmental needs in the future.

SCHEDULE APPROPRIATELY, STAFF ADEQUATELY Hospitals seek to attract staff by creating the most desirable and flexible schedules. Many nurses now work 12-hour shifts, which can create problems with patient continuity. Under such a schedule, the same nurse is not likely to care for the same patient from day to day, and this may aggravate problems with information exchange and can lead to medical errors.

The use of overtime, agency, and float nurses is problematic as well in that such personnel may be unfamiliar with the hospital, unit, and patients. Clinical staff must be knowledgeable, must be appropriately oriented to a unit and the hospital's policies and procedures, and must be free from unnecessary stress and fatigue.

Financial pressures on healthcare institutions often lead to staff reductions and replacement of registered nurses with less-skilled workers. Data overwhelmingly suggest that both quantity and quality matter when it comes to nursing care. See Sidebar N for the disadvantages of having an inadequate nursing staff.

Monitor Staff Effectiveness

JCAHO surveys hospitals' compliance with staffing effectiveness standards, including their selection of screening indicators. Fully implemented in 2003, these standards ask hospitals to discuss the following:

- the manner in which trends are tracked in screening indicators,
- the thresholds chosen to trigger an analysis of significant trends or variations in the data,
- the methods of analysis used to determine the contribution that staffing effectiveness has made to the variation, and
- the corrective strategies undertaken to address the findings.

A hospital should select a minimum of two clinical indicators that are relevant for and sensitive to all inpatients served. Such indicators can include adverse drug events, patient falls, skin breakdowns, patient injuries, and lengths of stay. Other indicators may be chosen to reflect unique patient populations.

Some hospitals may wish to collect indicators that are sensitive to some, but not all, inpatient populations. A minimum of two human resource indicators should also be selected, which may include nursing hours per patient day, overtime, sick time, staff satisfaction, staff turnover, and staff vacancy rate. Both direct and indirect caregivers should be included in the screening indicators. The human resources indicators may differ for each caregiver identified. Hospitals define which caregivers are included based on what impact the caregivers have on the chosen clinical screening indicators.

Hospitals must set goals for how they expect to perform for each of the indicators selected. Goals are then compared to actual performance to identify opportunities for improvement. Hospitals must capture and monitor data on the chosen indicators to identify patterns and trends in the data that may be related to staffing effectiveness. Data from multiple indicators should be displayed together in a matrix, table, or multiple line graphs. This way, potential relationships among the indicators are more readily identified.

If performance in any of the selected areas differs from that expected, hospital staff should analyze the data to identify the causes of variation. If deficiencies are noted, staff should develop and implement an action plan to promote improvement. Staff must keep hospital leaders informed about how staffing effectiveness affects performance, and leaders must demonstrate support for staffing-effectiveness activities.

A staffing effectiveness team may be established to assess and act on information as it is acquired. Staff should be accountable to ask "Why?" when data fall outside of acceptable performance, irrespective of whether the data relate to staffing. As data are analyzed, subgroups of the team can be charged with drilling down into the data and taking action between meetings. Bringing together human resources and clinical indicators allows questions about whether the staff mix is appropriate, whether the right person is in the right job, and whether the workload is appropriate.

Address Workforce Fatigue

Several high-profile incidents that involved fatigue of physicians in training have resulted in mandated maximum working hours for residency programs. Nurse fatigue and burnout need to be managed in a similar fashion. Some states have proposed legislation that forbids mandatory overtime for nurses, but these regulations do not address the issue of nurses who voluntarily work excessive hours.

Organizations must implement reasonable work schedules and must limit the total amount of hours that a nurse works. Managers or supervisors should provide sufficient breaks for staff. They should also recognize and make adjustments for overstressed employees.

Enhance the Environment

The current environment can be modified to improve working conditions and minimize error. Changes may involve adjusting lighting, noise, and workflow and eliminating clutter and other distractions.

Most nursing stations are cramped, leaving little space for either physicians or nurses to sit and carefully think about their patients or to document what transpired during the day. When transcribing orders, unit clerks are often distracted by the phone, family inquiries, or other interruptions. One option for ensuring that clerks can concentrate is to isolate them in another room while they perform their transcribing function. Volunteers may replace them in answering the phones and dealing with families until the clerks are finished with order entry.

Consider Clinical Processes

PROBLEM 1 The administration of hyperalimentation (high-calorie intravenous feeding) requires up-to-date information on a patient's fluid and electrolyte status and weight. Physicians may not have the time to write such orders, or the orders may be written before the day's laboratory results are reported. If laboratory studies are abnormal, expensive solutions may have to be discarded and new mixtures may have to be reformulated to correct the deficiencies.

PROBLEM 2 The dosage of certain antibiotics must be modified, depending on a patient's age and kidney function. Blood levels of an antibiotic may need to be drawn periodically throughout the day to assist in this determination.

Treatment delays can occur if the physician is not readily available or if the results are not promptly communicated.

Both of these clinical problems can be ameliorated by having the pharmacy staff assume responsibility for these tasks. Pharmacy should coordinate laboratory testing to improve outcomes and decrease errors.

Reduce Handoffs

The more handoffs between caregivers that occur during a patient care episode, the greater the likelihood of a mistake. Errors are possible in transferring orders, supplies, and information.

The medication ordering process is a prime example of a process that involves numerous handoffs and that presents many opportunities for errors. Physicians write orders; those orders are then taken off the chart by a nurse or technician and sent to the pharmacy, where other staffers review and fill the requests. Medications are then sent back to the unit for the nurse to distribute.

Computerized physician order entry (CPOE) eliminates some of the medication ordering steps that can lead to misinterpretations and errors. Four years after installing a CPOE system, Brigham and Women's Hospital in Boston experienced an 81 percent decrease in overall medication errors (Carter 2002).

Until an organization is able to implement a system such as CPOE, other simple and less-expensive steps can be taken to improve the quality of the handoffs that occur out of necessity:

- Require physicians to write all medication orders in block print.
- Instruct nurses not to attempt to interpret or guess on orders they cannot read. Instead, physicians should be contacted for clarification.
- Ask physicians whose handwriting is persistently poor to take a course to improve its legibility.
- Provide appropriate education, training, and monitoring to all involved in the medication ordering process.
- If possible, assign the pharmacy staff to input orders directly.
- Minimize verbal orders to the extent possible.

The simpler a procedure, the better the outcome. Every process in a healthcare organization is a candidate for simplification. Whenever a new policy or procedure is developed, a Failure Mode and Effects Analysis

(FMEA) can be used to define the worst-case scenario in the event of a breakdown in the technology or policy. See Sidebar O.

Employ Constraints and Forcing Functions

JCAHO's process for eliminating wrong-site surgery includes the constraint of a timeout—the surgery team takes time to agree on the nature of the procedure and the part of the body that needs the operation. Bar coding patient ID and medication ensures that a proper match is made before any medication is administered. Certain computer programs do not allow the input of data until all fields of information (e.g., allergies) are completed. Pop-up alerts on CPOE programs ensure that the physician thinks carefully about the medication that is being ordered and is made aware of potential untoward interactions with other medications or foods. Errors in blood transfusion are minimized by requiring two nurses to cross-check the patient with the ordered units of blood before administration.

Ask for the Help of Patient and Family

When possible, patients should be familiarized with their medications and should be encouraged to question the nurse if the medication or time of administration is not consistent with what they know. Families can also play a supportive role, being vigilant of their loved one's condition and notifying nurses if it has changed. They can also communicate important aspects of the patient's medical history, medication use, and allergies to the caregivers.

Although healthcare professionals may find it difficult to admit, they are aware that sometimes staffing on the unit may not be entirely adequate for patient's needs. The presence of a family member during certain hours of the day or night may promote greater patient safety, especially for the elderly patient who may be confused at night and thus be at risk for falls.

Encourage Teamwork

Unfortunately, some physicians still believe that they are at the center of the information network rather than one interdependent player in a complex system (Weick 2002). Physicians cannot function in the healthcare environment without a broad array of institutional supports, ranging from the medical records department to well-trained nurses. The patient needs a system that recognizes that each of its parts is interdependent. The effectiveness of the interactions among these parts determines the patients' outcome and satisfaction (Richardson and Corrigan 2003).

The best outcome for a patient is more likely if every health professional who works with the main physician is knowledgeable about the patient's illness and plan of treatment. This way, care is delivered accordingly.

Nurses are used to working in teams, sharing responsibility, and collaborating on decisions, but this style is uncommon with physicians. This philosophical gap may be the main reason that true collaboration between nurses and physicians is infrequent, and it must be bridged before teamwork can occur.

The following are areas in which teamwork does work:

- *Obstetrical unit*. The birthing process requires a good deal of coordination among caregivers. The physician must rely on staff to be his or her eyes and ears in the process.
- *Emergency department*. The substantial volume and intensity of most emergency departments (EDs) demand a considerable degree of coordination and understanding among physicians and staff. Otherwise, the work cannot be accomplished. Physicians are the scarce resource in the ED. They must depend on nurses to step in and take charge to ensure that patients are moving through the system, that changes in status are promptly and accurately conveyed, and that necessary analyses are completed in a timely manner.
- *Operating room*. Pockets of teamwork can be found in areas such as cardiac surgery, neurosurgery, and other specialties where the same staff work with the same surgeon on every case. In such instances, among the group there develops a comfort and an understanding of the procedures, resources required, and anticipated problems. Many more surgical cases may benefit from a team-focused approach.

Surgeons often find themselves working with staff they do not know and with staff who have never assisted with the procedure before. This is a frequent complaint of surgeons in light of staff turnover and the nursing shortage, and it has the potential to increase error.

It would be ideal at the minimum for the surgeon to meet with the staff before the case. At this introduction, the surgeon can learn about the individuals and their roles and then can explain the reasons for the procedure that will be undertaken, the findings and potential problems that may be encountered, and the particular needs the surgeon may have during the case. The operating room unit should do its best to ensure that qualified staff are assigned to the case, and, if possible, it should assign a mentor to assist a new nurse working on the case for the first time. Postprocedure debriefings can be helpful and can alert the staff and surgeon to any problems that need to be addressed before the next operation.

- *Case management.* Such a program provides the physician up-to-date progress on his or her patient's progress. Thus, it is helpful in developing the physician's sense that teamwork can make his or her life easier.

In addition, hospitals can encourage the development of stronger nurse-physician relationships on patient units by developing physician-nurse councils. These councils should meet regularly and give nurses and doctors an opportunity to discuss issues that not only affect patient care but also their working relationship (Spath 2000).

Address Medical Staff Quality Issues

Any organizational safety effort is likely to fail if it does not include physicians. But such efforts must overcome the medical profession's commitment to autonomy, self-regulation, and knowledge monopoly and everything that accrues from these essential characteristics, particularly suspicion and distrust of administrative incursions into medical territory. As hospital organizations have become more complex, managers more professional, and the external environments more demanding, the conflicts between physicians and managers have increased. The climate now is such that the medical profession finds itself increasingly challenged to address quality-of-care issues. Healthcare organizations can provide valuable assistance in these efforts.

PROVIDE TIMELY AND ACCURATE INFORMATION The good news is that physicians have an inherent desire to do what is best for their patients and to make care as safe as possible. What physicians need is accurate

information on which to base decisions about how to change patient care to improve outcomes. The challenge is determining where the problem lies: individual or system inadequacies or medical uncertainty. Physicians may be uncertain about their own knowledge and skills, the medical knowledge they use may be uncertain, and it may be difficult to distinguish between the two. In many instances of medical care, a course of action is only an error in retrospect. The physician may feel that what he or she decided to do was entirely reasonable given the information available at the time, even though the result was poor. On the other hand, a poor choice or wrong action may result in no patient harm. We need to be able to distinguish among the different types of mistakes and to recognize that not one correction fits all.

PREVENT NONPREVENTABLE EVENTS

Physicians and hospitals can work together on preventable adverse events such as wrong-site surgery, retained foreign bodies after surgery, and medication errors. They can also address all those errors currently designated as "nonpreventable," such as assumed irreducible minimums for complications such as an infection.

Improved technology or improved technique may solve some of these events, but unless these cases are considered critically, there is little chance for innovation (Rosenthal and Sutcliffe 2002).

REFINE THE CREDENTIALING PROCESS

An area that remains problematic for most medical staffs is the credentialing and recredentialing of physicians. The investigation of an applicant to a medical staff is generally thorough, especially if it is for a young practitioner who recently completed training. Obtaining the necessary documents and letters of recommendation required is relatively easy. Privileges are usually granted on the basis of those common skills learned in the particular training program.

Once a physician has been in practice for a period of time, these data become more difficult to retrieve. An organization that seeks information about a physician from another hospital most commonly only learns if the physician is "in good standing." The physician's sanctions or restrictions on his or her practice may be revealed as well, but that is a relatively infrequent event. It is difficult, if not impossible, to acquire any useful information about

SIDEBAR P

The National Practitioner Data Bank (NPDB) is designed to serve as a central source for information about physicians, providing data on malpractice payments, adverse licensure actions, adverse privileging actions, and professional membership restrictions. Hospitals must query the databank for every new applicant and at least every two years for other medical staff members. To make the data bank work, hospitals are supposed to report actions that involve reducing, restricting, revoking, or suspending clinical privileges of a physician for more than 31 days; any voluntary surrendering of privileges while under active review or in lieu of such a review; and any time, as a result of peer review action, a new or existing member of the medical staff is denied privileges. However, a study of clinical-privileges reports to the NPDB revealed that more than 65 percent of the surveyed hospitals reported no privileges actions from 1991 to 1995. The reasons suggested were that (1) there was an underdetection of physician with performance problems and (2) hospitals were employing penalties that did not require a report to the NPDB (Baldwin et al. 1999).

the quality of care practiced by the physician. See Sidebar P for the failure of one source of physician information—the National Practitioner Data Bank.

The NPDB is only one failure of the credentialing and recredentialing process. A larger problem is the inadequate assessment of the competence of physicians. Physicians are often recredentialed without a very vigorous look at the quality of care they provide. This is especially true if the physician practices at more than one hospital. Hospitals should require that physicians seeking to be recredentialed and who work primarily at another facility provide a list of patients and of procedures

and outcomes that are sufficient for the department chair and credentials committee to recommend reappointment.

A physician's privileges should also be periodically reviewed and adjusted, depending on experience and outcomes. Physicians who rarely care for patients with a particular diagnosis or who infrequently perform a high-risk procedure should be asked to voluntarily withdraw such privileges. Unfortunately, many physicians currently maintain the same privileges for the duration of their tenure at a hospital, regardless of experience or outcomes. Recredentialing based on assessment of physician competence can be contrasted with the requirement that airline pilots demonstrate their competence every six months (Leape, Swankin, and Yessian 1999).

Hospital executives must challenge medical staff leaders to review the current credentialing and recredentialing processes for latent deficiencies and to make appropriate adjustments. The board must be more involved in evaluating this process as well. Developing a subcommittee of the board may be useful. This subcommittee can review recommendations from the credentials committee and medical executive committee before physician credentials are brought forward to the full board for a vote.

This requires that the hospital provide the necessary resources for accurately tracking in-hospital outcomes. The medical staff can then use such data during recredentialing cycles. In the past, hospitals have relied on medical staffs to acquire these data and to perform the appropriate reviews. This is clearly not happening to any significant degree in U.S. hospitals. Physicians do not have the time to acquire, organize, and analyze such data; therefore, it is incumbent on the organization to do so. Including this type of tracking necessitates a major organizational commitment from the organization to broaden its quality resource management activities.

REFERENCES

Aiken, L. H., S. P. Clarke, D. M. Sloane, J. Sochalski, and J. H. Silber. 2002. "Hospital Nurse Staffing and Patient Mortality, Nurse Burnout, and Job Dissatisfaction." *Journal of the American Medical Association* 288 (16): 1987–93.

Baldwin, L. M., L. G. Hart, R. E. Oshel, M. A. Fordyce, R. Cohen, and R. A. Rosenblatt. 1999. "Hospital Peer Review and the National Practitioner Data Bank: Clinical Privileges Action Reports." *Journal of the American Medical Association* 282 (4): 349–55.

Bogner, M. S. 1994. "Human Error in Medicine: A Frontier for Change." In *Human Error in Medicine*, edited by M. S. Bogner, 379. Hillside, NJ: Lawrence Erlbaum Associates.

Carter, C. L. 2002. "Following Orders?" *Alliance* (July): 8–12.

Ethicon. 2003. [Online information; retrieved 9/03.] http://www.ethicon.com/page/about /credo.html.

Feldman, S. E., and D. W. Roblin. 2000. "Accident Investigation and Anticipatory Failure Analysis in Hospitals." In *Error Reduction in Health Care: A Systems Approach to Improving Patient Safety*, edited by P. L. Spath, 141. San Francisco: Jossey-Bass.

Healthcare Business Roundtable. 2000. "Reducing Medical Errors, Improving Patient Safety." *Healthcare Business*, Special Supplement, July.

Helmreich, R. L., and A. C. Merritt. 1998. *Culture at Work in Aviation and Medicine*, 133–135. Burlington, VT: Ashgate Publishing Co.

Issenberg, S. B., W. C. McGaghie, I. R. Hart, J. W. Mayer, J. M. Felner, E. R. Petrusa, R. A. Waugh, D. D. Brown, R. R. Safford, I. H. Gessner, D. L. Gordon, and G. A. Ewy. 1999.

"Simulation Technology for Health Care Professional Skills Training and Assessment." *Journal of the American Medical Association* 282 (9): 861–66.

Johns Hopkins Quality Update. 2003. *Walking the Talk of Patient Safety.* Newsletter, Issue 1, August.

Joint Commission on Accreditation of Healthcare Organizations (JCAHO). 2002. *Sentinel Event Alert*, June 17. Oakbrook Terrace, IL: JCAHO.

Kaplan, T. 1998 [Online information; retrieved 8/03.] *The Tylenol Crisis: How Effective Public Relations Saved Johnson & Johnson.* http://www.personal.psu.edu/users/w/x/wxk116/tylenol/crisis.html.

Lamb, R. M., D. M. Studdert, R. M. Bohmer, D. M. Berwick, and T. A. Brennan. 2003. "Hospital Disclosure Practices: Results of a National Survey." *Health Affairs* 22 (2): 73–83.

Leape, L. L., D. S. Swankin, and M. R. Yessian. 1999. "A Conversation on Medical Error." *Public Health Reports* 114 (4): 302–17.

Luciano, L. 2000. "A Government Health System Leads the Way." In *Reducing Medical Errors and Improving Patient Safety: Success Stories from the Front Lines of Medicine*, 9–11. Washington, DC: The National Coalition on Health Care, The Institute for Healthcare Improvement.

Miller, G. A. 1956. "The Magical Number Seven, Plus or Minus Two: Some Limits on Our Capacity for Processing Information." *The Psychological Review* 63 (2): 81–97.

Milstein, A. and N. E. Adler. 2003. "Out of Sight, Out of Mind: Why Doesn't Widespread Clinical Failure Command Our Attention." *Health Affairs* 22 (2): 119–127.

National Aeronautics and Space Administration (NASA). 2003. [Online information; retrieved 12/03.] http://asrs.arc.nasa.gov/overview.htm.

Needleman, J., P. Buerhaus, S. Mattke, M. Stewart, and K. Zelevinsky. 2002. "Nurse-Staffing Levels and the Quality of Care in Hospitals." *New England Journal of Medicine* 346 (22): 1715–22.

Reason, J. 1997. *Managing the Risks of Organizational Accidents*, 17; 107–24. Burlington, VT: Ashgate Publishing Co.

Richardson, W. C., and J. M. Corrigan. 2003. "Provider Responsibility and System Redesign: Two Sides of the Same Coin." *Health Affairs* 22 (2): 116–18.

Rosenthal, M. M., and K. M. Sutcliffe (eds.). 2002. *Medical Error: What Do We know? What Do We Do?* 237–64. San Francisco: Jossey-Bass.

Sharpe, V. A., and A. I. Faden. 1998. *Medical Harm: Historical, Conceptual, and Ethical Dimensions of Iatrogenic Illness*, 31. Cambridge, England: Cambridge University Press.

Spath, P. L. (ed.). 2000. *Error Reduction in Health Care: A Systems Approach to Improving Patient Safety.* San Francisco: Jossey-Bass.

Weick, K. 2002. "Reduction of Medical Errors Through Mindful Interdependence." In *Medical Error: What Do We Know? What Do We Do?* edited by M. M. Rosenthal and K. M. Sutcliffe, 186. San Francisco: Jossey-Bass.

Wilson, N. J. 2000. *Strategies for Leadership: An Organizational Approach to Patient Safety.* Irving, TX: VHA Inc.

Wilson, N. J., and M. J. Hatlie. 2001. "Advancing Patient Safety: A Framework for Accountability and Practical Action." *Journal for Healthcare Quality* 23 (1): 30–34.

Conclusion

The handling of an airplane crash is starkly different from the management of a major adverse event in the hospital. Immediate actions by the airline industry following an airline crash are instructive to healthcare with respect to error prevention.

Minutes after the crash, all major news networks are reporting relevant information—the airline involved, number of passengers and fatalities, and origin and destination of the flight. Later, the public learns about the aircraft model and its history of problems and maintenance, the pilot and copilot and their experience, and the crew onboard. Eventually, the contents of the black box may be revealed as well as the final transmission of the pilots. A formal report is ultimately issued that states the likely cause of the accident. If evidence is found that a particular model has a possible defect, all airlines are instructed to inspect their specific aircrafts; in severe cases, all airplanes of such type may be grounded pending further review.

Overall, every citizen knows almost as much about the crash as the investigators do. The upshot of this approach to an adverse event is that airline travel today is safer than driving, and people are more confident that they will reach their destination safely when they get on a plane.

The airline industry, however, did not always do such a good job. In the late 1970s, research determined that 70 percent of the crashes were caused by human error as opposed to equipment malfunction or weather disturbances. The majority of errors among airplane crews consisted of leadership failures, poor coordination, or deficient decision making. The industry sought to improve the psychological training of its crews, focusing on their leadership skills, communication, and group dynamics. Such training has been expanded to include others beyond the cockpit, and this is now known as crew resource management. Statistics show this improvement. In the 1970s, 1 fatal accident occurred in every 140 million miles flown on a commercial jetliner. In 2003, deadly crashes occur in 1 every 1.4 billion miles (Boeing 2003).

Captain Dan Maurino of the International Civil Aviation Organization noted:

It is sad that it had to take accidents before existing knowledge, which might have been applied pro-actively to prevent unnecessary pain and destruction called aviation's attention to cultural factors.... Our outcome-oriented professional culture demands that the system be broken before we start thinking about fixing it (Helmreich and Merritt 1998).

The reason for this inaction is that safety is a dynamic nonevent. Lack of adverse outcomes does not mean that nothing is happening. A safe system is one in which people understand that they must be mindful of both interrelationships and unexpected occurrences. Weick and his colleagues (2002) investigated what they termed "high-reliability organizations" and found a unique manner in which people in these institutions related to each other and to their work:

When they interrelated their separate activities, they did so heedfully.... Their heedful interrelating also was reflected in the care they directed toward accurate *representation* of the other players and their contributions...and...was evident in...*subordinating* their idiosyncratic intentions to the effective functioning of the system.... When interrelating was done heedfully, there was an increase in the alertness and intelligence that was mobilized to deal with the unexpected. And errors decreased. The resulting *mind* of this system...did not lie inside the head of any one person. Instead, the mind was located between people, in the quality of their relating.

This is the kind of mind-set we all need to bring to healthcare to make the culture of safety a reality.

Medical error and patient safety need to be approached from a systems perspective. As Eric Trist (1983) noted, "complex societies in fast-changing environments give rise to sets or systems of problems (meta problems) rather than discrete problems. These are beyond the capacity of single organizations to meet. Interorganizational collaboration is required...."

The current fragmentation of the health "system" makes such interorganizational collaboration unlikely, except at the most general level. Organizations can respond to policy and procedure mandates from JCAHO, CMS, and others. However, the individual organization remains responsible for addressing its own internal quality and safety issues with its available personnel and resources.

REFERENCES

Boeing. 2003. [Online information; retrieved 12/03.] http://www.boeing.com/commercial/safety/pf/pf_howsafe.html.

Helmreich, R. L., and A. C. Merritt. 1998. *Culture at Work in Aviation and Medicine*, 133–35. Burlington, VT: Ashgate Publishing Co.

Trist. E. 1983. "Referent Organizations and the Development of Inter-organizational Domains." *Human Relations* 36 (3): 269–84.

Weick, K. 2002. "Reduction of Medical Errors Through Mindful Interdependence." In *Medical Error. What Do We Know? What Do We Do?* edited by M. M. Rosenthal and K. M. Sutcliffe, 193. San Francisco: Jossey-Bass.

Appendix A

Strategies for Leadership:
Hospital Executives and Their Role in
Patient Safety

complete?		Personal Education
Y	N	
		Read *To Err is Human: Building a Safer Health System,* Kohn LT, ed, Corrigan JM, ed, Donaldson MS, ed. Washington, DC: National Academy Press; 1999.
		Read other primers on patient safety: • *Human Error*, Reason, JT, Cambridge University Press, 1990. • *The Psychology of Everyday Things*, Norman, D, Basic Books, 1988. • *Managing the Risks of Organizational Accidents*, Reason, JT, Ashgate Pub. Co., 1997. • *Normal Accidents: Living with High Risk Technology*, Perrow, C, Basic Books, 1984. • Lucian Leape's seminal articles.[1] • *Human Factors in Aviation*, Wiener, EL, Nagel, DC (eds), Academic Pr, (1989).
		Participate in external safety education programs, CME, conferences, etc.
		Hold detailed conversations with in-house experts on our realities of practice.
		Walk my hospital with a human factors expert.
		Walk my hospital as a patient.
		Familiarize myself with enhanced JCAHO Patient Safety Standards.[2]
		View Bridge medical video "Beyond Blame"[3] and Partnership for Patient Safety video "First Do No Harm."[4]

This document is reprinted with permission from Jim Conway. Dana-Farber Cancer Institute, Boston, MA.

complete?		Call to Action *Modeling the way...Mobilizing the effort*
Y	N	
		Speak publicly to various audiences on the unacceptability of the current state of and my commitment to patient safety as a personal and corporate priority. Include safety focus in hospital publications, stategic plans, etc. • Board and hospital leaders • Medical and hospital staff • Patients/consumers • Media
		Implement a proactive effort on patient safety design, measurement, assessment, and improvement. Include direct care, administrative and clerical staff, and patients and family members in all aspects.
		Set the goal of establishing an environment of trust with a non-blaming, responsibility-based approach to the causation of incidents and errors; establish policy in this area.
		Set the expectation for timely and interdisciplinary error and near-miss investigations with an emphasis on: patient/family impacted by the error; the broader institutional implications of and learning from the error; and the support of staff at the sharp end [closest to care].
		Build quality improvement and patient safety policies into staff orientation and continuing education offerings.
		Set the expectation for executive involvement in significant incident investigations.
		Establish a policy to ensure patients/families are notified ASAP when an error reaches a patient.
		Establish effective grievance systems for patients/families who see themselves as "victims of error."
		Establish mechanisms to train leadership and other experts in patient safety.

complete?		Practicing a Culture of Safety
Y	N	
		Openly engage with medical staff, nursing, and other leaders in patient safety planning.
		Continuously articulate the business case for safety improvement.
		Personally participate in a significant incident investigation/root cause analysis.
		Tell "my story" around incidents/errors that I have been involved with and the systems improvements that could have prevented them.
		Routinely involve myself, all levels of our staff, and our patients and family members in direct and ongoing communications around the patient safety work of our institution and areas for improvement.
		Routinely bring patient safety matters, trending data, and specific cases to the board and other hospital leadership committees.
		Routinely probe staff perceptions of risk areas from existing or proposed systems and take immediate actions wherever possible.
		Openly support staff involved in incidents and their root-cause analysis.
		Ensure that there is ongoing prioritization and achievement of safety improvement objectives.
		Ensure that articles on patient safety matters regularly appear in my organization's communications vehicles.
		As part of annual budget preparation, ensure resources are funded for priority safety areas.
		Request and routinely receive reports on facility utilization of and comparison with best-practice information from the AHA,[5] NPSF,[6] and ISMP.[7]
		Ensure self-assessments from the AHA and others are completed and used internally for quality improvement activities.
		Cultivate media understanding of patient safety and my organization's efforts to improve safety.
		Ensure effective systems are in place to assess individual accountability and competence.

complete?		Advancing the Field
Y	N	
		Share my personal and the institution's patient safety learning outside of the organization.
		Participate in local, regional, and national conferences, coalitions, and other efforts to improve patient safety.
		Engage in initiatives to drive enhancements in regulatory, facility/ professional licensing, and accreditation agencies that support safety improvement and cultural change in consort with the specific goals of the agency.
		Advocate for my professional association to make/keep patient safety a high priority.

Next Steps *Action Items to Get to "Yes"*

Short-term Goals:

Long-term Goals:

NOTES

[1] Publications of Lucien L. Leape and colleagues:

"The nature of adverse events in hospitalized patients: Results from the Harvard Medical Practice Study II," Leape, L. L., Brennan, T. A., Laird, et al. New Engl J Med, 1991, 324:377–384.

"Error in medicine," Leape, L. L. JAMA, 1994. 272:1851–1857.

"Systems analysis of adverse drug events," Leape, L. L., Bates, D. W., Cullen, D. J., et al. JAMA, 1995, 274:35–43.

"Out of the darkness," Leape, L. L., Hlth Sys Rev, 1996, Nov/Dec 21–24.

"Promoting patient safety by preventing medical error," Leape, L. L., Woods, D., Hatlie, M., et al., JAMA, 1998, 280:1444–1447.

"Why should we report adverse incidents?," Leape, L. L., J Eval Clin Pract, 1999, 5:1–4.

"Safe health care: Are we up to it?," Leape, L. L., and Berwick, D. M., BMJ 2000, 320:725–726.

"Reducing adverse drug events: lessons from a breakthrough series collaborative," Leape, L. L., Kabcenell, A. L., Gandhi, T. K., et al., Jt Comm J Qual Improv, 2000, 26:321–331.

[2] The revised standards are available at the JCAHO web site at http://www.jcaho.org /ptsafety_frm.html

[3] Order through Bridge Medical at http://www.mederrors.com

[4] Order through the Partnership for Patient Safety at http://www.p4ps.org

[5] Reference American Hospital Association safety site at http://www.aba.org /medicationsafety/medsafety.asp

[6] Reference National Patient Safety Foundation site at http://www.npsf.org

[7] Reference Institute for Safe Medication Practices site at http://www.ismp.org

Appendix B

Strategies for Leadership:

An Organizational Approach to Patient Safety

Instructions	
Step 1	Because patient safety is a complex multidisciplinary topic, it is recommended that each health care organization establish a multidisciplinary team to complete a single organizational assessment. The team should consist of a minimum of six individuals drawn from a sufficiently broad pool of key decision makers. A team should include at least two representatives from each of the following categories: • Direct care providers *(physicians, nurses, pharmacists, respiratory therapists, etc.)* • Middle management *(service chiefs, head nurses, supervisors)* • Top management *(senior executives, chiefs of staff)*
Step 2	Have each team member completely review the organizational assessment before beginning the self-assessment process. Then as a team, evaluate your current status in implementing the associated activities. Choose responses that apply to your specific facility even if your facility belongs to a larger health care system. If necessary, discuss the status of the activities with other members of your organization who may be in a better position to assess the degree of implementation. When a consensus on the level of implementation has been reached, place an "X" in the appropriate box using the scoring key at the top of each page. *Note: For questions that include multiple components, full implementation (scores of 4 or 5) should be recorded only if all components have been fully implemented. If only partial implementation of all components has occurred or if only one of several components has been fully implemented, record your score as a 3.*
Step 3	Have each team member complete the overall summary questionnaire on page 8. Next, sum your total scores and compare with the results of the overall summary. (Maximum score is 270 [54 items x 5].) The team should identify three to five low scoring activities and develop an action plan to move them closer to full implementation in all areas of the organization. Use this organization assessment tool annually to monitor your improvement.
Step 4	Complete the accompanying demographics if you plan to compare your results to other facilities or health care systems.

Note: Questions regarding this tool can be directed to VHA's Keith Kosel at (972) 830-0684 between 8:30 AM – 5:30 PM (CST).

VHA gratefully acknowledges the methodology and content contributions of The Institute for Safe Medication Practices that were used in producing *An Organizational Approach to Patient Safety* tool.

I. LEADERSHIP

A There has been **no discussion** around this activity.
B This activity is **under discussion, but there is no implementation.**
C This activity is **partially implemented in some or all areas of the organization.**
D This activity is **fully implemented in some areas of the organization.**
E This activity is **fully implemented throughout the organization.**

Key Aspect of Safety:	*Demonstrate patient safety as a top leadership priority.*	none	partial		full	
		A	B	C	D	E
Patient safety is adopted as a strategic goal by the organization and the governing body.						
Senior leadership allocates resources to accomplish patient safety initiatives.						
Risk management, quality management, and patient advocacy are functionally integrated around advancing patient safety.						
One committee or senior leader oversees patient safety within the organization.						
Leadership regularly monitors progress in implementing the patient safety agenda.						
Leadership promotes patient safety in the larger health care community through new and established associations.						
All departments, services, and standing teams/committees apply safety principles to work deliverables.						

Key Aspect of Safety:	*Promote a non-punitive culture for sharing information and lessons learned.*	none	partial		full	
		A	B	C	D	E
The organization has a non-punitive policy to address patient adverse events involving medical staff and organization employees.						
Leadership encourages and rewards recognition and reporting of adverse events and near misses.						
Senior leadership, the medical staff and organization employees address patient adverse events with courage and honesty, looking for system issues to improve and lessons to share across the organization.						
The activity of legal counsel is aligned with the patient safety agenda to ensure consumer, public, and legal accountability, while concurrently protecting the organization.						
Senior leadership directly communicates with medical staff and employees using case studies that illustrate a non-punitive approach to adverse events.						
Senior leadership, medical staff and organization employees role-model non-punitive attitudes that emphasize system failure rather than individual error in clinical teaching and quality review conferences, such as morbidity and mortality conferences.						

II. STRATEGIC PLANNING

A	There has been **no discussion** around this activity.
B	This activity is **under discussion, but there is no implementation.**
C	This activity is **partially implemented in some or all areas of the organization.**
D	This activity is **fully implemented in some areas of the organization.**
E	This activity is **fully implemented throughout the organization.**

Key Aspect of Safety:	*Routinely conduct an organization-wide assessment of the risk of error and adverse events in the care delivery process.*	none	partial		full	
		A	B	C	D	E
An organization-wide patient safety assessment occurs at regular intervals.						
The organization uses the safety assessment results to develop a written Patient Safety Plan.						
The Patient Safety Plan is reviewed and approved by the governing body, medical staff, legal counsel, and senior leaders annually.						
The Patient Safety Plan includes tactics to build a safety awareness campaign.						
There is a contract management process that evaluates the capabilities of suppliers to meet patient safety requirements.						

Key Aspect of Safety:	*The organization actively evaluates the competitive/collaborative environment and identifies partners with whom to learn and share best practices in clinical care.*	none	partial		full	
		A	B	C	D	E
Lessons learned from health care and from other industries are incorporated into the Patient Safety Plan.						
The organization routinely engages the consumer community in a proactive dialogue about safety.						

III. INFORMATION & ANALYSIS

A	There has been **no discussion** around this activity.
B	This activity is **under discussion, but there is no implementation.**
C	This activity is **partially implemented in some or all areas of the organization.**
D	This activity is **fully implemented in some areas of the organization.**
E	This activity is **fully implemented throughout the organization.**

Key Aspect of Safety:	*Analyze adverse events and identify trends across events.*	none	partial		full	
		A	B	C	D	E
The organization offers all employees and medical staff a user-friendly, easily accessible, confidential, narrative reporting system for recognized risks, near misses, and adverse events.						
Following an adverse event, quality improvements are identified, implemented, and monitored for effectiveness.						
Trends across events are regularly identified and used to drive quality improvement priorities.						
Patient safety intelligence from sources such as compliments; complaints; patient, employee, and medical staff satisfaction data; and claims is integrated in quality improvement planning.						
Adverse event analysis is conducted by those knowledgeable in human factor design principles (e.g., hindsight bias).						
Evidence-based measures are used to monitor and improve performance toward zero-defect care for high-risk and high-volume conditions and diseases.						
Employees and medical staff report issues or occurences impacting patient safety.						
There is a safety alert communication and dissemination system that gets information to the right people in a timely fashion.						

IV. HUMAN RESOURCES

A	There has been **no discussion** around this activity.
B	This activity is **under discussion, but there is no implementation**.
C	This activity is **partially implemented in some or all areas of the organization**.
D	This activity is **fully implemented in some areas of the organization**.
E	This activity is **fully implemented throughout the organization**.

Key Aspect of Safety:	*Establish rewards and recognition for reporting errors and safety driven decision-making.*	none	partial	full		
		A	B	C	D	E
The organization explicitly defines employee and medical staff roles in advancing patient safety in job descriptions, orientation, and required continuing education.						
All employees complete continuing education in patient safety and quality management.						
Following a patient safety adverse event or near miss, stress debriefing is provided using peer counselors or other means.						
Following a patient safety adverse event or near miss, the person involved is provided non-punitive management support.						
Making safety driven decisions is an essential element of the reward and promotion system.						

Key Aspect of Safety:	*Foster effective teamwork regardless of a team member's position of authority.*	none	partial	full		
		A	B	C	D	E
Training and practice is provided to support employee competencies in required new and existing clinical and interactive team skills.						
Simulation is used to improve interpersonal communication and team interactions in high-risk settings.						
Medical staff bylaws and regulations require continuing education and practice to maintain competencies in required new and existing clinical and interactive team skills.						
Leadership empowers employees, regardless of rank, to act to avoid adverse events.						
The organization maintains safe staffing through such activities as cross-training, adequate volume ratios, appropriate skill mix, and limited work hours.						
Education and career development plans foster core competencies of continuous performance improvement, direct and open communication, innovation, and problem solving.						

V. PROCESS MANAGEMENT

A	There has been **no discussion** around this activity.
B	This activity is **under discussion, but there is no implementation**.
C	This activity is **partially implemented in some or all areas of the organization**.
D	This activity is **fully implemented in some areas of the organization**.
E	This activity is **fully implemented throughout the organization**.

Key Aspect of Safety:	*Implement care delivery process improvements that avoid reliance on memory and vigilance.*	none		partial		full
		A	B	C	D	E
The organization uses checklists, protocols, reminders, decision support, and standardizes equipment, forms, times, and locations to avoid reliance on memory in acheiving zero-defect care.						
The organization uses system constraints, forcing functions, natural mapping, and effective alarms to avoid reliance on vigilance in achieving zero-defect care (e.g., IV luer lock and indwelling lines match beflore fluid can be infused; when a device fails, it defaults to the safest mode).						
Patient care processes use a minimum number of steps and handoffs.						
Patient care processes are designed with built-in opportunities to recover from critical error (e.g., reversing agent for overdosing of medication).						
Patient care processes are designed such that safe, zero-defect care requires minimum effort to deliver.						
Process redesign is piloted prior to widespread implementation to identify new sources of process failure and/or adverse events resulting from the change.						
Process redesigns are monitored for effectiveness.						
The organization invests in information technology to support patient's safety (e.g., computer order entry, decision suport).						
The organization seeks active input from end users of technologies, supplies, and products prior to purchase.						
Technologies, supplies, and products are piloted by end users prior to widespread implementation.						

VI. PATIENT & FAMILY INVOLVEMENT

A	There has been *no discussion* around this activity.
B	This activity is *under discussion, but there is no implementation*.
C	This activity is *partially implemented in some or all areas of the organization*.
D	This activity is *fully implemented in some areas of the organization*.
E	This activity is *fully implemented throughout the organization*.

Key Aspect of Safety:	*Engage patients and families in care delivery workflow process design and feedback.*	none	partial		full	
		A	B	C	D	E
Mechanisms are in place for immediate response to patient and family-reported safety measures.						
Patients and families are actively involved in planning services, work/process design, problem solving, and quality improvement efforts.						
Patients and families receive information and education they need to be full partners in their care (e.g., evidence-based guidelines, personal medical data, self-management instructions, etc.).						
Patient information and education is designed and delivererd in useful formats and matched to literacy and cultural needs.						
The organization informs and apologizes to patients and their families when an adverse event occurs.						

Suggested Readings

Bogner, M. S. (ed.). 1994. *Human Error in Medicine*. Hillside, NJ: Lawrence Erlbaum Associates.

Casey, S. 1993. *Set Phasers on Stun and Other Tales of Design, Technology, and Human Error*. Santa Barbara, CA: Aegean Publishing Co.

Helmreich, R. L., and A. C. Merritt. 1998. *Culture at Work in Aviation and Medicine*. Burlington, VT: Ashgate Publishing Co.

Kohn, L. T., J. Corrigan, and M. S. Donaldson (eds.). 2000. *To Err Is Human: Building a Safer Health System*. Washington, DC: National Academy Press.

Reason, J. 1990. *Human Error*. Cambridge, England: Cambridge University Press.

———. 1997. *Managing the Risks of Organizational Accidents*. Burlington, VT: Ashgate Publishing Co.

Rosenthal, M. M., and K. M. Sutcliffe (eds.). 2002. *Medical Error: What Do We Know? What Do We Do?* San Francisco: Jossey-Bass.

Rubin, S., and L. Zoloth. 2000. *Margin of Error*. Hagerstown, MD: University Publishing Group.

Sharpe, V. A., and A. I. Faden. 1998. *Medical Harm: Historical, Conceptual, and Ethical Dimensions of Iatrogenic Illness*, 29–31. Cambridge, England: Cambridge University Press.

Spath, P. L. (ed.). 2000. *Error Reduction in Health Care: A Systems Approach to Improving Patient Safety*. San Francisco: Jossey-Bass.

Vaughan, D. 1996. *The Challenger Launch Decision*. Chicago: University of Chicago Press.

Weiner, E., B. Kanki, and R. Helmreich. 1993. *Cockpit Resource Management*. Philadelphia, PA: Academic Press.

About the Author

Matthew J. Lambert, III, M.D., M.B.A., FACHE, is senior vice president of clinical operations at Elmhurst Memorial Hospital in Elmhurst, Illinois. Dr. Lambert has been a physician and surgeon for over 35 years and has spent 16 years in healthcare administration. He has served as medical director of Martha Jefferson Hospital in Charlottesville, Virginia, and as vice president for medical affairs at St. Joseph Health Centers and Hospital in Chicago. In addition, he was senior vice president for medical affairs at Catholic Health Partners, a multihospital system in Chicago.

Dr. Lambert's work has focused on clinical quality improvement and error reduction as well as operational process improvement and innovation. He is also experienced in the cultural transformation of organizations and in leadership development. He has codirected the Physician Executive Boot Camp for the American College of Healthcare Executives.

Dr. Lambert is a Fellow of both the American College of Surgeons and the American College of Healthcare Executives. He served as associate professor of surgery at the University of Virginia School of Medicine in Charlottesville. Dr. Lambert received his bachelor of science degree from the University of Notre Dame in South Bend, Indiana, and his doctor of medicine degree from St. Louis University in Missouri. He completed his surgical training at the University of Michigan Medical Center in Ann Arbor.

He can be reached at mlamber @emhc.org.

Acknowledgments

It is a privilege to have the opportunity to write a book about so important a topic as the reduction in medical error and the development of a culture of safety. I am most appreciative to Tom Atchison for recommending me to Health Administration Press (HAP) for this project and to Audrey Kaufman and Jane Williams at HAP for guiding me to its completion.

I am indebted to many professional colleagues—physicians, nurses, and healthcare executives— who have shaped my career and my commitment to improving the quality of patient care. I specifically acknowledge the staff at Martha Jefferson Hospital in Charlottesville, Virginia, where many of my ideas took root and where I first embarked on a second career in healthcare administration.

I express my gratitude to Sister Theresa Peck and the staffs of St. Joseph Hospital and Catholic Health Partners, both in Chicago, for giving me so many wonderful opportunities to learn about organizational dynamics and about building relationships with other organizations. My current position at Elmhurst Memorial Healthcare allows me to work with a dedicated group of board members, executives, nurses, physicians, and employees. Together, we work to improve and innovate hospital operations to reduce error and improve patient safety. My special thanks to Leo Fronza, CHE, president and CEO of Elmhurst Memorial Healthcare, for his leadership and dedication to excellent patient care.

Finally, all I am as a person I owe to two very special sets of people. My parents, Matt and Fran Lambert, started me on a lifelong journey of inquiry through their encouragement of reading and learning. They remain two of the most interesting and vigorous people I know, and I love them dearly.

My wife, Donna, has supported and encouraged me for the past 25 years, as I explored new territories and new careers. She has been the driving force behind all of my efforts and the reason for any success I have enjoyed. She has been a partner for the ages, and I only wish I had a thousand more years to spend with her. Our children, Matthew and Kate—one a musician, the other an actor—have made it all worthwhile and have helped me realize what life is really all about.